Integrated Storytellii by Design

This pioneering work equips you with the skills needed to create and design powerful stories and concepts for interactive, digital, multi-platform storytelling and experience design that will take audience engagement to the next level.

Klaus Sommer Paulsen presents a bold new vision of what storytelling can become if it is reinvented as an audience-centric design method. His practices unlock new ways of combining story with experience for a variety of existing, new and upcoming platforms. Merging theory and practice, storytelling and design principles, this innovative toolkit instructs the next generation of creators on how to successfully balance narratives, design and digital innovation to develop strategies and concepts that both apply and transcend current technology.

Packed with theory and exercises intended to unlock new narrative dimensions, *Integrated Storytelling by Design* is a must-read for creative professionals looking to shape the future of themed, branded and immersive experiences.

Klaus Sommer Paulsen is an award-winning concept developer, designer, storyteller and creative director. His expertise in the convergence of storytelling, digital innovation and experience design has been built through a career spanning decades and disciplines. He has collaborated with VIA University College Film & Transmedia, Aarhus University, University of Southern Denmark and University of Tartu Pärnu College. He was also the contributing editor of Create Converge's 2019 anthology *Storytelling Beyond The Screen*.

Integrated Storytelling by Design

Concepts, Principles and Methods for New Narrative Dimensions

Klaus Sommer Paulsen

Routledge
Taylor & Francis Group

LONDON AND NEW YORK

First published 2022
by Routledge
605 Third Avenue, New York, NY 10158

and by Routledge
2 Park Square, Milton Park, Abingdon, Oxon, OX14 4RN

*Routledge is an imprint of the Taylor & Francis Group,
an informa business*

Library of Congress Cataloging-in-Publication Data
Names: Paulsen, Klaus Sommer, 1970- author.
Title: Integrated storytelling by design: concepts, principles and
    methods for new narrative dimensions / Klaus Sommer Paulsen.
Description: New York, NY: Routledge, 2021. | Includes
    bibliographical references and index. |
Identifiers: LCCN 2020058235 (print) | LCCN 2020058236 (ebook) |
    ISBN 9780367856991 (hardback) | ISBN 9780367856977 (paperback) |
    ISBN 9781003014454 (ebook)
Subjects: LCSH: Storytelling. | Narration (Rhetoric) | Marketing.
Classification: LCC PN4193.I5 P38 2021 (print) |
    LCC PN4193.I5 (ebook) | DDC 808.5/43—dc23
LC record available at https://lccn.loc.gov/2020058235
LC ebook record available at https://lccn.loc.gov/2020058236

ISBN: 978-0-367-85699-1 (hbk)
ISBN: 978-0-367-85697-7 (pbk)
ISBN: 978-1-00-301445-4 (ebk)

Typeset in Bembo
by KnowledgeWorks Global Ltd.

Access the companion website: IntegratedStorytellingByDesign.com

TO ANJA
0707

Contents

Futurecasting

Afterword

Acknowledgements

I am very proud to have my name on the cover of Integrated Storytelling by Design as its author. However, it is not just the result of my efforts, but also of those who have helped out, given advice and supported me from idea to completion. I owe thanks to so many fine people, some of which I would like to acknowledge on the pages of the book that they also deserve some credit for.

THANK YOU!

My wife Anja for not just being patient with me while I was working on this book, but also encouraging me to get to work on it … and get back to work on it.

Ecaterina Capatina for her dedication to the principles in this book, never-ending support, cover art direction, illustrations, research and so much more.

Inga Krasovska and Diana Kichukova for additional illustrations.

Annette Corpuz Breum for additional research.

Katherine Kadian, Alyssa Turner, Emma Tyce and the rest of the team at Taylor & Francis for believing in Integrated Storytelling by Design and help shaping it.

Joe Pine, Guy Gadney, Fri Forjindam and Jason Bruges for taking the time to discuss and inspire. You are all true masters of your respective fields.

Laurence Beckers, Hugh Gledhill, George Kelion, Matt Barton and Lars Vesterlykkegaard for granting access to use of visuals of some wonderful work.

Shawn J.H. Lee for his beautiful cover art.

Everyone who have joined the Integrated Storytelling sessions and discussions online or on locations around the world. It was a pleasure and an inspiration to spend time with you whether you were in the beginning or well into your career.

All who have shown an interest in this book, which has kept me motivated to keep on going, not at least through the challenges presented by 2020. I hope you find it worth the wait.

And finally, thanks to you for picking up Integrated Storytelling by Design! I hope it will be as inspiring to read and work with, as it was putting it together.

Introduction

"To know that we know what we know, and to know that we do not know what we do not know, that is true knowledge."

Nicolaus Copernicus

CHAPTER 1

Enter the new world of storytelling by design

The idea and concept for this book came about from working in the inspiring and innovative borderland of themed and branded entertainment and experiences. This is where the stories truly become experiences, and these experiences become memorable moments, worth retelling again and again as stories in their own right. Further depth was added by sharing the insights learned through practice as applicable theory at university lectures, professional training, talks and presentations on the methods and models collected in this book. What began as practical application for creative development became the foundation for a set of principles and practices to integrate storytelling with experience design for not just attractions, entertainment and Experiential Marketing, but across many different industries and markets. After all, we find ourselves in a new golden age of storytelling. We are all living our own stories, on both a personal and professional level.

The power of the story and the experience, and the convergence of the two into a new discipline, has gained foothold across multiple industries, as they have proven to be applicable and valuable for a wide range of uses. They are still very relevant to those working in, or aspiring to work in, the entertainment industry, whether we are talking movies, games, theme parks or something else. However, as learning, healthcare, marketing, retail, urban development and other industries that have arguably not been considered as part of The Experience Economy[1] recognise the impact of the audience experience and narrative, both strategies and practical methods are needed to establish new and other kinds of connections and relationships between them and the people they want to reach. As a testament that its applicability reaches beyond destinations, attractions and entertainment, Integrated Storytelling has been used in one form or the other for branding, design and development for IT services, hardware cooling systems, community building, farming, business acceleration programs, learning, wellness and beauty products to name just a few. Not only does this show the width of the relevance of the principles of this book, but how storytelling and experience design is evolving as strategic initiatives and capabilities needed by an ever-increasing number of organisations, whether they define themselves as commercial or not.

> Storytelling and experience design is evolving as strategic initiatives and capabilities.

The next step in the evolution of the narrative comes from combining storytelling with design processes to create new ways of developing and experiencing the story. There is a need for a creative and strategic concept that enables those who understand and apply it, to create a convergence and consequent reinvention of story-related disciplines through new ways of developing narrative structures; creators no longer merely tell a story, they design a story experience.

> Creators no longer merely tell a story, they design a story experience.

This book is intended to be the toolbox for all the storytellers wanting to move forward on this particular path of innovation and play their role in the evolution of storytelling, regardless of what industry they see themselves related to. It is based on the premise that as the story and the experience converge and evolve, narratives become story experiences that integrate and are integrated across platforms, disciplines, media, technologies and organisations with an audience-centric approach, keeping the audience at the centre of the story experience universe. As the storyteller becomes a creator and designer of story experience, new disciplines and methods are needed.

The principles in this book have been developed for years, and combine and integrate design thinking, storytelling, integrated marketing, creative strategy and experience design into a new 'Storytelling by Design' discipline: Integrated Storytelling. At its core, it combines story and experience to be able to create something new that can be structured and connected with the audiences in multiple ways across various engagement points. The stories come alive in a wide range of forms and variations, that is, how they are presented in combination with how they are experienced. As a creator's toolbox, Integrated Storytelling by Design consists of a range of principles and models that brings a design perspective to story structures to

> Integrated Storytelling by Design consists of a range of principles and models that brings a design perspective to story structures.

help the creation of Integrated Storytelling projects from early creative strategy through concept to the design, production and the real-time delivery of the final experience. It is valuable to keep in mind, though, that Integrated Storytelling is also a mindset, without which the models merely become exercises in formula without depth or real significance. It is the heart of the story experience design and creation.

On a note regarding terminology, the word **audience** is consistently used throughout this book for anyone whom the story experience is created for; users, visitors, customers, gamers, etc., all share the same definition here, while stile noticing that their wants, needs and characteristics are different. However, rather than defining the audience by the above-mentioned designations, modalities and roles are applied to them, as someone may be a customer at one point, and a visitor at another point – even within the same location and within a short timeframe.

The various modes that are represented during a day at an attraction or a retail mall are prime examples of spaces that can benefit from accommodating different needs and roles. In visiting time spanning minutes, hours or days, most will be involved in different tasks and activities, such as eating versus shopping and taking versus immediately going to the next ride. The new roles and the appreciation for the audience being active, passive and in particular modes during their engagement in the story are explored as a fundamental part of the principles in this book. Integrated Storytelling, as a design method, includes a very nuanced and dynamic view on what audiences are, individually or in groups. Audiences are more than segments or target groups. They are real people with real hopes, fears, dreams, wants and needs. As an active audience, they also have functions and modalities, levels of engagement and immersion. Even more so, they have a role to play within the story experience.

> Audiences are more than segments or target groups.

Integrated Storytelling by Design represents a journey from storyteller to story designer, taking storytellers and designers alike into new and sometimes uncharted lands that keep evolving, sometimes in mysterious and surprising ways. This book is not intended to be the final definition of Integrated Storytelling or the related disciplines that would be presumptuous as the evolution of the story experience is in constant flux and development. At every class, presentation and talk, those participating have been invited to join the campfire, where the evolution of story experiences is discussed; we are nowhere near the end of what they can become. Anyone reading this book and applying its principles should recognise that even though it is designed for longevity and relevance, their journey and that of Integrated Storytelling does not come to a conclusive stop here.

This is where it begins.

NOTE

1. Pine, B.J. and Gilmore, J.H.: *The Experience Economy*, Updated Edition (2011).

CHAPTER 2

Structure

Integrated Storytelling by Design is presented in seven main parts that introduce and explore the principles and methods of Integrated Storytelling to build a comprehensive understanding of what the concept is and how it can be applied.

In immediate continuation of this chapter about the structuring of this book, twelve fundamental principles and elements for creating Integrated Storytelling experiences are listed, and they are explored in depth at later points in the book. Listing them like this at this point of the book ensures that they will always be readily available and summarised, and thus be useful regardless of whether the book is being read in a printed or digital version. It is a point of navigation for accessing whether the book is being read in part or full, or being used as a toolbox while designing new narratives.

Each of the seven structural parts of Integrated Storytelling by Design consists of descriptions, models and practical applications. The practical applications can be used for reflection or assignments to exercise the methods. Named 'From Theory to Practice', these segments are intended to do just that; bridge the theories and models to practical use.

Case examples are mostly concentrated in Part 7 of the book. Additional case content can be found on the companion website IntegratedStorytelling.com.

CHAPTER 3

Seven key components of Integrated Storytelling by Design

Integrated Storytelling by Design begins with the first three parts dedicated to the dynamic of an evolving and, thus, changing relationship between the creator, the story and the audience significant to the design of new narrative experiences.

Part I: Story explores how the aeons-old influence from audiences creating living, responsive storylines has evolved with the audience now being able to interact with and influence the story experience in real time from anywhere in the world. The concept of Integrated Storytelling is introduced, and an example of a concept that has transcended technologies for more than a hundred years is presented. Spoiler alert! It features little, not-so-green men from Mars.

Part II: Design takes elements from storytelling and reinvents and realigns them as design objects, creating one part of the bridging that is needed to develop themed or branded experiences where story and experience design come together as one. An essential part of this is a design method that truly allows creators and designers to invite audiences to enter their storyworlds – the short term for a narrative universe full of multiple storylines and characters – and become part of the story.

Part III: Audience is dedicated to the actual stars of Integrated Storytelling; the audience. In this part of the book, it is explored how a new, more nuanced view on the audience and their engagement with storytelling in any format opens up for new ways of creating narrative experiences that evolve with the engagement of the audience; either influences each other. This part of the journey from a storyteller to a story designer also presents further dimensions to consider regarding design and what interaction may be able to unlock. It addresses the question of whether a story can be interactive; it is not a question of **if** it can be, but **how** it can be interactive.

Part IV: Experience bridges with Part I: Story in order to create a design approach that merges story and experience at a deeper level to establish conceptual anchoring points where the story, contradictory to common understanding, does not necessarily have to precede the experience. Designing experiences predates such IT-related disciplines as user experience and interaction design; however, they too play a part in the convergence of design principles needed to create truly cross-disciplinary creations. The continuing inclusion of new kinds of experiences and interaction development is the basis for a more holistic approach to experience design, one that now also includes story experience design, the discipline of merging storytelling with experience design to focus on the experience of the story over the mere delivery of it.

Part V: Convergence is dedicated to the importance of the multiple layers of Integrated Storytelling coming seamlessly together to create and maintain a harmonious construction. The audience may only see and encounter the tip of its surface, but the success of the project lies in it being well integrated in depth and width, both as a concept and as a finished creation that people will experience. As the term itself implies, integration is not just one thing, but dependent on perspectives of those who are in front of or behind the proverbial curtain.

Part VI: Creation contains important considerations and pointers for the story creator about to embark on an Integrated Storytelling project. Defining a creative strategy, assessing the project and testing the story experience are included in Part VI without going excessively into the deeper details of project planning and management; there are plenty of good titles addressing this in depth, some of which are included in the literature list. The Creation part is wrapped up with a cautionary note on the power and the responsibilities that story creators have, both of which are becoming increasingly evident in today's world of communications and miscommunications overload. the power to change Narratives have the power to change the minds and actions of individual people, groups and mobs. It is nothing new that their impact can be further amplified with transformative experiences. Now this can happen anywhere, anytime, beyond fixed locations and specific hours. With great power comes great responsibility, and storytelling *is* very powerful.

Part VII: Application is a collection of various ways of applying Integrated Storytelling to multiple industries, as the principles are being applied to many other industries other than themed and branded entertainment. The various applications include marketing, brand experiences, retail, game design, museums and others, with cases exemplifying how Integrated Storytelling principles are applied in real-life projects.

This is far from an all-encompassing list of possible variations, as Integrated Storytelling is continuously being adapted either in principle

or as a named concept by an increasing number of organisations representing a growing number of industries. The companion website
IntegratedStorytelling.com will be updated with new cases from different sources and creators as the projects they represent become public.
Furthermore, everyone using the principles in this book is encouraged to
submit their project through the website.

Integrated Storytelling by Design concludes with a look at how to
predict the future of storytelling. What may define the future of the story?
The exact prediction is not included, but ways of uncovering it are. It is
a roadmap for anyone to make their own prediction about what may lay
ahead. You are encouraged to explore it and share what you may find with
others.

CHAPTER 4

Design principles and elements of Integrated Storytelling

In order to successfully develop new story experiences that work within the new dynamic of the creator, the story and the audience, a set of principles of and methods takes the concept of Integrated Storytelling from overall idea to design and application.

They build on and sometimes challenge the established rules and models of telling stories, presenting the content of media and the design of experiences, enabling the merging of the story with the experience in new ways. In doing so, they open up the storyworld to the audience, to not just observe or explore the world of the narrative, but to ultimately enter and change storylines or even create them.

Each of these design principles will be explored further in the chapters of this book, with the practical From Theory to Practice assignments provided to take them from theoretical models to practical application.

Story Sphere

The Story Sphere is made up of everything that the audience encounters as they journey through our story experience designs. It effectively places them in the centre of our storyverse, if they accept the invitation to enter. It has different layers that enable more nuanced choices regarding audience levels of influence and interaction, such as not if, but how, a story can be interactive.

Learn more on page 69

Modular Storytelling

Modularisation of storylines enables the creator to work with them as elements in a design structure that can be assembled, scrambled and realigned in many different ways to provide a multitude of new story variations. In a successful design, the audience experienced a convergence of modular elements rather than fragments. Modularity is the principle that enables a dynamic structure of Micro Stories and Micro Experiences alike.

Learn more on page 80

Micro Stories

Micro Stories are the building blocks of Modular Storytelling, wherein each of the elements can work on their own or together in linear or random order. The principle of Micro Stories allows for stories with no specific middle and sometimes no – or no singular – end of a story and can be used in the design of tales that learn made possible by artificial intelligence.

Learn more on page 77

Audience programming

To engage with the audience that travels, explores and interacts with the elements in our Story Spheres, designers and creators need a more nuanced view and understanding of their audience; a perspective that goes beyond segmentation and target groups and takes a new look at the people we are trying to reach. Recognising that we are all creatures of code with a programming that influences perceptions and actions helps define new groups of audiences, and how we see their role.

Learn more on page 93

Audience roles

A monumental shift in the understanding of the audience is driven by realising the change in their roles and their level of influence to the storyline. It is a role that needs to be considered in any case, as the audience is already more empowered than what most training in storytelling, media and communications has prepared creators for. Adding to the complexity, the roles are not static and may be in flux even as the audience travels through the Story Sphere. The change may occur over minutes as well as hours or days. Designing with audience roles adds another layer of a design narrative, and even helps to avoid having the story, the audience and the experience elements conflict due to over-complexity or incompatibility. Each has to be properly integrated and balanced based on the intended state of the audience.

Learn more on page 114

Contextual audience design

Similar to working with the existing and new roles of the audience, the context in which they engage with the story experience needs to be taken into serious consideration. Locations, modalities and levels of engagement are among the conditions that affect the audience experience, and how people can or will act and interact. For a successful, holistic story experience design, context has to be a primary consideration and utilised as part of the design, even at the core of the content framed within.

Learn more on page 129

Memory coding

Design for themed and branded experiences, or what can be defined as creative experience design compared to IT-related user experience design, is about the creation of memorable moments. When aspiring to do so, there may be pre-existing memories to take into consideration; the imprint or the coding of new memories does not always happen on an empty canvas. Furthermore, types of memories are different, and the memory imprint can be created in a multitude of ways. We are all creatures of code, and memory programming and deprogramming is an effective way of actively using this insight as part of the story experience design.

Learn more on page 146

Modular Experience Design

The memory of an experience is a convergence of more than just one event, and what many consider as one event is actually made up of different elements. This allows for designing experience as a combination of modules, which establishes a direct link to the modularised story. As Modular Experience Design mirrors that of the Modular Story Design, the two may blend, not at least when seen and felt through the eyes and minds of the audience.

Learn more on page 144

Micro Experiences

Mirroring the Modular Storytelling building blocks, Micro Experiences are the equivalents to Micro Stories, i.e., a set of smaller events that can be experienced in different ways and order to create an individual, unique memory for groups and individuals alike. The type and level of depth of each experience may differ to build the dynamic of an experience narrative with highs, lows and whatever lies in between.

Learn more on page 143

Contextual Experience Design

The context and the space in which the experience design comes alive is an integral part of the memory that is being created. Here, the audience roles and modalities take on a new meaning, as mutual influence and functions are taken into consideration to truly immerse the audience in the story experience. The Contextual Experience Design both mirrors and adds to the Audience Context Design, and just as the case with modularity for stories and experiences may come together as one, the same may happen with contextually for the audience and the experience.

However, considering them as two different perspectives adds to variation such as experience locations and audience types to ensure a connection with the place where they take place. Furthermore, interactions and user design principles come into play in terms of navigating audience the audience in understanding missions and directions, as when moving forward assisted by signs or other means of wayfinding.[1]

Learn more on page 161

Horizontal and vertical integration

There are two axes to the integration of all the elements that make up the story experience. One is the width and reach of integration; platforms, story modules, space, time, etc. The other is the depth of integration; how deep can the audience dive into one point, and how deeply is it rooted in the place or brand it represents. Furthermore, how well is it supported beneath the surface or behind the stage by the organisation that is tasked with bringing the story experience to life? The first is named as the horizontal integration, the latter as the vertical integration. To succeed, both the width and the depth needs to be properly weighted in combination in a larger, integrated design and implementation structure.

Learn more on page 172

The integrated experiential narrative

Every element and design consideration converges into an experiential narrative. It is an immensely powerful platform for cross-disciplinary understanding of the occurrences of the story experience design. It is a step-by-step description of how everything unfolds in front and around of the audience through their point of view, as they travel through and engage with the elements of the narrative elements. Regardless of discipline or role, every team or cast member can use the integrated experiential narrative to define their individual roles and tasks within a shared context and consensus.

Learn more on page 170

A combination of principles

Summing up the 12 design principles, it should be noted that Integrated Storytelling is more than the sum of its parts. Every story experience designed and created is a unique combination made up of the creator, audience and story dynamic and the design principles above. Constructing and combining these elements in dynamic ways makes up the balance and convergence that makes each Integrated Storytelling experience lives up to its full potential as a unique, rich design.

NOTE

1. Wayfinding refers to systems that guide people through a physical environment and enhance their understanding and experience of the space.

Part I
Story

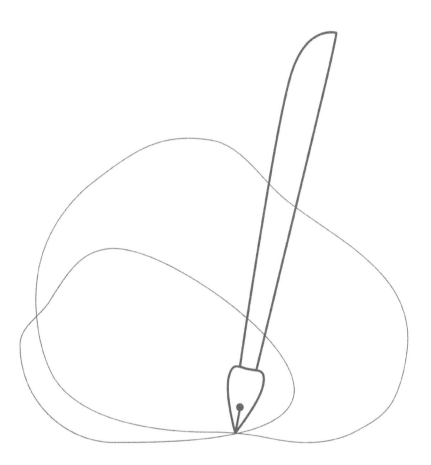

"Speech belongs half to the speaker, half to the listener."
Michel de Montaigne

CHAPTER 5

The rise, fall and rise
of the living story

What is storytelling? If you are a storyteller, what kind of storyteller are you? As storytelling evolves in new, intriguing and sometimes seemingly mysterious ways, the future of the story may not be telling it but bringing it to life in various innovative ways. The true revolution in storytelling is the new relationship between The Creator, The Story

The true revolution in storytelling is the new relationship between The Creator, The Story and The Audience.

and The Audience, regardless of whether the creator is a representative of a discipline such as writing, moviemaking, game development, content marketing or themed experience design.

We are past the linearity of the creator presenting a static story to their audience; rather, any of the three parts influences one another. In Integrated Storytelling, the role of new technology, new format, innovation and invention is to support this dynamic, even if hidden out of plain sight of the audience.

Nearing the full potential of this new dynamic, the art and craft of storytelling have come to the next point of evolution. A milestone that is not only initiated by the many digital possibilities available to the storytellers, but also by the adaption of – and confidence – on the part of the audiences in using platforms for interacting with, influencing, creating and distributing stories themselves.

New technologies and spaces shared between the creator and the audience are advancing the very fabric of story structures forward, building a need for new narrative models or updated versions of existing ones. At first, it may be hard to fully grasp how ground-breaking this movement forward to the next step truly is. However, it cannot be ignored by storytellers of any kind, regardless of whether they are studying or teaching the craft or are aspiring or established professionals. The world of storytelling is becoming more than what it was, which will open up new challenges and opportunities.

We are already witnessing the first waves of what storytelling is going to become, with social media, co-creation and narratives transformed into immersive experiences, showing signs of what is to come. Gazing into the crystal ball, what awaits may be stories that seemingly come alive, capable of learning from and adapting to their audiences with no need for an author to edit or rewrite them. The story and real-time interaction with it are now simultaneously integrated in specific places and distributed worldwide to an unlimited number of locations.

> The story and real-time interaction with it are now simultaneously integrated in specific places and distributed worldwide to an unlimited number of locations.

There may be more than one space, and not just the story, but the interaction with it can happen from anywhere. The world is the stage in which a multiverse of storyworlds grows.

STORYTELLING WITH POWER AND PURPOSE

Storytelling is part of the foundation of what makes up and has made up the connection that binds together humans from a handful of people in the earliest families from the dawn of time to the prehistoric tribes that settled in villages and finally established civilisations. Stories have conveyed messages, values and beliefs from one generation to the next for aeons. It has immense value for the community for sharing its culture between individuals and for each individual to understand his or her place in the world. The stories we share define and describe our values, dreams, fears and aspirations, and add to both personal and group narratives of who we are. They are fundamental representations of identity.

Thus, when the power of storytelling is addressed, it does not only concern the capacity of creating moments of entertainment or messages of marketing; it builds opinions, persuasions and beliefs, political as well as religious, progressive as well as aggressive towards those of different beliefs. Wars have been waged and heroes have been immortalised with written words or visual depictions of their quests and conquests. Progress in science and society has been inspired by visions and made possible by knowledge shared, and superstitions and urban legends have had their backward effects even in a modern society because of the powerful way their stories have been presented. Stories have the power to inspire people to take action for the better, as well as the power to seduce and blind them to the point of taking part in questionable, even despicable actions.

Driving all of the above forward, there have always been the dynamics of the relationship between the storyteller, the story, the presentation and the audience. From the earliest days of congregating around the campfire, these elements in combination have made up the storytelling experience for the audience. A great concept and an excellent presentation have always been able to move the mountains of human persuasions and beliefs. Whether presented by a tribe sage tens of thousands of years ago or by a TED speaker after their opening up to the public in 2009,[1] creating a connection with the audience is what makes the message or the morale come alive with persistence.

Some would say it takes more than images and words, but sometimes the presentation can do with less. It all comes down to the power of the message or the power of the story. Some of the best speakers in history have not used visual representation other than their own presence and spoken words to create unparalleled dynamics with the audience: Martin Luther King Jr., Gandhi and John F. Kennedy all stand as proof that the presentation can be carried without flashy visuals when the message is strong and resonates with the masses. In contrast, less convincing talks prove the opposite; that a weak message or story cannot be made stronger by even the most spectacular presentation.

> A weak message or story cannot be made stronger by even the most spectacular presentation.

This also rings true in many current storytelling experiences, where the postproduction wrapping and effects are more developed than the concept and the storyline. The point is that we can throw as much technology and glitter at our story experiences, but in the end, their success with audiences all depend on strong concepts, story and experience alike.

A HISTORY OF IMAGES, WORDS AND BEYOND

The oral storytelling traditions that were conceived by our ancestors would most likely have allowed for change – even on the spot – by the storyteller, for him or her to gain, retain and build on the interest and fascination of the audience. The ability to improvise would enable the storyteller to adapt a narrative to its audience, meaning that the audience could have a direct influence on the storyline. The spoken story would become an organic entity, a living storyline that would evolve during and after the interaction with the audience, ensuring the storyteller's grip on the tribe or their settlement simultaneously.

The living story

The concept of a living story is not exclusive to Integrated Storytelling. It has been defined as being embodied in not just the person, but in tribes, communities and tribal communities. It has been stated that we live out the 'living story' in our daily lives,[2] and the 'living story' takes on a life all its own, and lives through us. The idea of a living concept is not exclusive to academia, either, as it is used by consultancies, studios and agencies for responsiveness, adaptability and even to the point of using it as a company name.

In the context of Integrated Storytelling, however, the living story is to be seen as a narrative entity that is not only lived by people or used as the basis for improvisation. As an organic concept, the living story allows the influence of audiences, particularly in real time, which makes the story, and how it is experienced, a dynamic outcome of an interaction between the story and the audience. The story experience may be scripted and designed, but the true, final form is not shown before it is interacted with.

> The living story allows the influence of audiences, particularly in real time, which makes the story, and how it is experienced, a dynamic outcome of an interaction between the story and the audience.

With new technology, this interaction and mutual influence can now happen directly between the audience and the story itself, making the story, metaphorically spoken, come alive. Adding online technology, this influential interaction can even happen at the same time from anywhere around the world. For the first time ever, the audience, the creator and the story are not limited by distance or other physical confinements. The responsive story experiences have become ubiquitous, but not necessarily universally similar.

Visual mediation

The earliest examples of the living story becoming visualised and more or less static through depiction are the cave paintings and drawings created tens of thousands of years ago; such as the 42,000-old depictions of seals found in Spain or the preceding non-figurative nine red lines found in South Africa, dating as far back as 73,000 years.

The illustrations could still act as a scene for the prehistorical storyteller, but the big leap was that the audience could experience the story without

Prehistoric drawing in cave at Lascaux.

the narrative presented by an appointed individual, especially when the art represented recognisable scenes like hunting woolly mammoths.

Some of the story concepts and elements we use today have been engraved in our collective human consciousness from the time of the cave paintings. One example of this is the 'The Venus and The Sorcerer' in The Chauvet-Pont-d'Arc Cave, Southern France, with its depictions of its archetypical titular characters accompanied by a beastly character. Three entities that have been encountered in an almost endless number of fairy tales, myths and legends throughout the history of humankind, leading up to the contemporary success of Harry Potter and his kin. Part of the reason why the magical tale of the young wizard resonated so well with so many is that the understanding of and connection with his world was already there.

PRINT MEDIATION

With the invention of books and printing, invented first by the Chinese, then evolved further with replaceable letters by Gutenberg in 1450, a revolution in storytelling began. Due to the sheer scale of replication and distribution made possible, the number of printed books and consequently, new titles started to grow considerably. As did their readership and the impact of ideas and knowledge being shared widely.

As the production of books became streamlined to successfully encapsulate one singular form of presenting the storyline, it became less organic and influenced by the audience. The words were printed. They became static, compared to the dynamics of a living story. It can be rightfully argued that children's books and religious books were open to the same kind of interpretation and presentation as in the times before the era of the printed when someone presented them to an audience who could not necessarily read the words themselves. However, the story itself would remain just as it was printed. Obviously, there were essential edits and congregated versions published, to make earlier versions obsolete or to be dismissed; but with print mediation, the immediate influence from the audience was no longer present. The story became a static construction.

> With print mediation, the immediate influence from the audience was no longer present. The story became a static construction.

Movie mediation

With the invention of Thomas Edison's phonograph in 1987 and the release of Roundhay Garden Scene directed by French inventor Louis Le Prince in 1988, the era of sound and motion pictures effectively began; the latter adding moving images to the story. The story itself was still fixated, even more so with sound and pictures being produced once to be played back multiple times in a specific way.

Distribution platforms Multimedia mediation

On 2 November 1920, KDKA in Pittsburgh, Pennsylvania, received the first US radio broadcasting license; even though it did not start regular broadcasting in 1921, this marked the beginning of century of electronically distributed media. It would eventually culminate with ubiquitous online media access that makes it possible to receive and publish content from anywhere to anywhere. The live stream from the broadcast meant that news, messages and stories could now be acted out and presented live, to be experienced at home. Just a few years later, in 1928, the first US television station WRGB started to broadcast, and soon both images and words could be presented live in the home of the audience.

Throughout the twentieth century, a wide range of media was established and adopted by a mainstream audience, each of them with their unique characteristics. Some of them were relevant for a few years, just to be merged with, being developed further into or replaced by something else. The home video revolutionised the way people watched movies but were rendered obsolete by DVDs that were barely surpassed by Blu-Rays before digital video and streaming became a standard for movie watching. The sales of vinyl records dropped to the point of only a few factories back with the capability to produce them when CDs were introduced. Then this new format was overtaken by digital versions and streaming, with vinyl records surprisingly making a comeback in the twenty-first century. The media evolution – or rather, revolution – has continued to affect books, comics, movies and other formats as digital devices and the use of them continued to evolve.

Regarding storytelling, the vast array of media platforms provided many different platforms for a narrative unfold. The audience could see the movie, and then read the comic. Or, read the book, and then see the movie. Or, see the movie, and then play the game.

CREATOR-CENTRIC DISTRIBUTION PLATFORMS

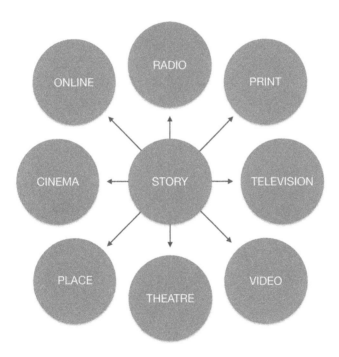

With the main work as the centre of the story universe – a book, a film, a comic, etc. – each of the media platforms could have its unique version that was anchored in the main work. Sometimes, the story would be the same but produced for another platform, such as comic book adaptions of movies. Other times, a story on a new platform would have nothing to do with the main narrative and would be disregarded as part of a franchise's canon. One example is some of the dreadful video game adaptions of movie franchises, or in reverse, dreadful movie adaptions of video game franchises. The story universe with the main story in the centre can be depicted as a series of platforms that each have their individual storyline, which can sometimes be combined with more or less success. Other times, they will – often unintentionally – appear utterly disconnected, which underlines the need for connections points and integrated story design and development.

AUDIENCE-CENTRIC ENGAGEMENT PLATFORMS

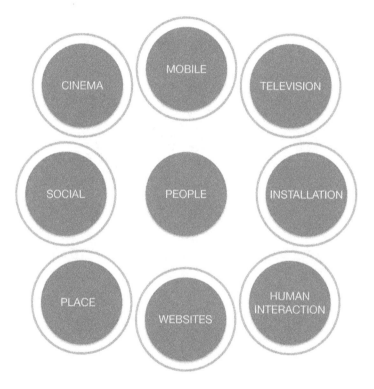

With mainstream access to computers and then the internet, the audience has advanced to be more than consumers. They have become users, increasingly empowered by choice and capability. If they do not find something interesting, they will quickly click away. If they want to create and share, the explosion of social media sharing platforms has enabled them to do so without any need for further technical insight. As the audience are now used to this empowerment – which is arguably sometimes taken too far – the story and the storyteller are no longer the centre point

> The story and the storyteller are no longer the centre point of the relationship and dynamic between the creator, story and the audience.

of the relationship and dynamic between the creator, story and the audience. The audience is the centre point, and because of this momentous shift, we need to think differently about how we tell and deliver stories. Not only is the story distributed through various platforms. Its relevance is defined by the rate of engagement with the audience across each platform.

With the audience at the centre point of a storyverse that is shared with the platforms, the audience journey sets the direction for which platforms are relevant to use and what content should be added to them. The barrier between the audience,

> The barrier between the audience, the story and the platform is non-existing, and interaction and influence with the narrative has become a natural way to experience a story.

the story and the platform is non-existing, and interaction and influence with the narrative has become a natural way, to experience a story. There is not necessarily a specific order of when and where the audience engages with the story through any particular platform. In the past, the comic book adaptations of movies were a way for the audience to relive the stories of those movies. Now, one can easily revisit the movie and any other representation of the storyverse. Some content that would usually be experienced on different platforms as books, movies and games may now all be presented together on devices such as digital tablets, making the jump from one to the next a simple one. Which all drives the convergence of ways of entering the story's universe into a combined transmedia, multimodality experience. See the movie, read the book, play the game, all accessed with a single device.

It does not make sense to replicate the same storyline all the time, as there is room to elaborate and differentiate from one platform instance to the next, with more connected and complex storyverses will be created. Rather than each platform having its unique version of a storyline, they all become part of a larger storyverse, where each platform represents a unique perspective or storyline. Everything and anything can be part of the storyverse, which means that in development and production, story creators have to have the capability of moving from multidisciplinary storytelling to interdisciplinary storytelling. They need to advance from being able to create story experiences on multiple platforms to creating story experiences that combine the platforms, and, in doing so, apply existing disciplines in new ways.

All of this calls for new ways and levels of integrated story creation. The evolution of the audience role and experience dictates that the role of the storyteller changes, as the discipline branches out and the term story creator or story designer becomes more fitting to the task. Various platforms, formats and purposes will be among the new avenues explored. By applying design thinking and principles, a new foundation can be built for a new generation of living stories, rooted well in the new relationship between the creator, the story and the audience.

A dynamic, in which the audience, empowered by the balancing of new technology and design principles influences how storylines, and as such, storytelling, evolve.

NOTES

1. Chris Andersen: TED Talks: The official TED guide to public speaking (2018)
2. David M. Boje: What is Living Story Web? (2012/2018)

CHAPTER 6

The concept of Integrated Storytelling

ADVANCING THE EVOLUTION OF THE STORY FROM TELLING STORIES TO DESIGNING STORY EXPERIENCES

The themed entertainment industry, with its attractions, theme parks, museums and other themed spaces, is the epicentre of most principles of translating stories into experiences, and the saying here is that the magic begins with the story. At the core of every Disney or Universal theme park, visitors will find a wealth of well-known franchises such as the beloved animated Disney classics, Harry Potter, Star Wars and the Marvel Universe. The theme parks made the stories come to life as immersive environments and experiences, long before anybody was even thinking of digital games with extensive virtual environments. Historically, the story was often already established in one format or the other, be it books, films or comics, before making its way into the physical world. For it to maintain relevance and become worthy of multi-million-dollar investments, the story had to show longevity and wide-spread appeal, proving that it was a great story set within a fascinating storyworld that could stand the test of time. In return, reconstructing the story in real life added to its longevity, establishing a symbiotic, mutually empowering relationship.

The same applies to a great extent today, with some of the most significant investments in the attractions industry being based on hugely successful, well-established story franchises, creating a symbiotic at-home and out-of-home experience. In these scenarios, the media and the themed attractions feed off each other's success and relevance; watch the story at home or at the cinema; live the story at the theme park. With digital games, the story as interactive experience has made its way into the homes and personal devices of the audience, enabling both at-home and out-of-home interactive entertainment to be platforms within a story universe.

The groundwork has been done to prepare for new hybrids of interactive storyworlds that stretches across time, space and disciplines, adding gamification to physical spaces, and more in-depth storylines to interactive experiences. These hybrids merge the disciplines of experience design and storytelling to a higher degree, in which story franchises – or IPs[1] – are being developed specifically for story-based experiences with a cross-disciplinary, holistic approach rather than establishing the story first with the audience, and then design the experience.

> The story-experience design hybrid is evident at the heart of many upcoming, innovative concepts from the beginning.

The story-experience design hybrid is evident at the heart of many upcoming, innovative concepts from the beginning. One example of story and experience being developed simultaneously is the world's first non-linear interactive dark ride[2] Popcorn Revenge[3] that opened in 2019 at the Walibi theme park in Belgium. With the opening of the ride, an IP was from its very beginning designed as a combination of story development and experience design, with neither outranking the other.

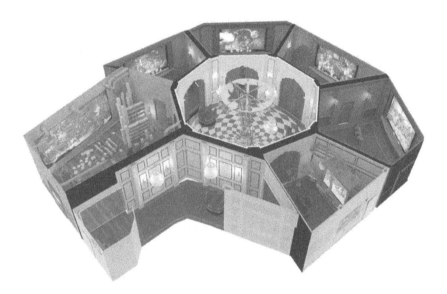

Popcorn Revenge makes it possible to enter different rooms and missions in random order.

©Alterface.

Popcorn Revenge's central mission room.

©Alterface.

There are also quite a few successful IPs in the gaming industry, in which the story is being explored as a deeper, more integrated part of the overall experience, rather than merely being used for cut-scenes or other connection points between one gaming sequence and the next. One notable franchise is The Last of Us, for which the creators have gone to great depth with character development to create a deeper connection with the on-screen characters, making the audience care more about the lead characters' fate in a post-apocalyptic world.

For concepts like Popcorn Revenge and The Last of Us, the story and the experience need to be perfectly balanced in a way that may change dynamically throughout the ride or the game. Either represents the need for the capability to create new, interdisciplinary and interactive story-worlds, characters, as storytelling in the twenty-first century is evolving into a new range of story experiences. It is often claimed that the magic begins with the story, but will this stay true? Or, does it begin with the story and the experience at the same time, with two things happening at once being part of the magic? With Integrated Storytelling, the two merges at the concept stage. It is not done by magic; it is made possible by design. Part

It is often claimed that the magic begins with the story, but will this stay true?

of the process is to make certain that both the story and the experience consists of strong components. With one being the story, as we move from storytelling to story experience design, we still have to ask ourselves: what makes a great story?

THE MAKINGS OF GREAT STORIES

To reverse-engineer and rearrange stories, first they need to be viewed as constructs based on narrative structures containing various elements such as characters, props and spaces placed in storylines moved forward by plots and subplots from beginning to end. Sometimes, the mechanics of storytelling are invisible to the audience; sometimes, they are not. When the elements become visible when not intended, the story experience may be significantly poorer; as in situations where a character is no longer perceived as a believable person, but as an actor portraying a character in an unbelievable wat. When telling a story, regardless of format, evoking curiosity, emotion and immersion is necessary to bring the audience to a state of suspension of disbelief, during which they let down their mental guard and accept the combined story elements as a second reality. Then, they willingly choose to look past the logic that what they see are actors, props and set design in a constructed reality to allow them all to be part of seemingly real events in a seemingly real world.

To the audience in this state of mind, the lead actors are the protagonists and the antagonists, the storylines are intriguing events, the props are deadly weapons or magic items and the reader, viewer, listener – the audience – are transported through time and space to a world within the universe that frames the story. This is not just limited to story experience created for audiences of books, movies, television or comics, but extends into both the themed experience in the physical world and the gamer's digital reality and beyond. When you are in a well-designed Transformers ride, you are battling the Decepticons. When you are making your way through the Wild West in Red Dead Redemption 2,[4] your journey and struggles become real, and your controller becomes whatever tool or weapon you have chosen to win the day. When you enter an open-air museum, you are transported to another place and another time. Furthermore, when the museum crosses over into applying theatrical and theme park principles to enhance the experience, the people or, rather, the cast members, you meet are real persons from the period, you find yourself transported.

All story creators need to be aware of the dynamic between them and their audience. Once the audience has reached a state of suspension

Den Gamle By (The Old Town) is an open-air museum where visitors interact with cast members in character.

Den Gamle By (The Old Town Museum).

of disbelief, a mental contract has been accepted. Breaking it will push those engaged with it towards leaving the story behind in frustration. People in general and dedicated fans alike may decide to abandon story franchises and associated story-based

> Once the audience has reached a state of suspension of disbelief, a mental contract has been accepted. Breaking it will push those engaged with it towards leaving the story behind in frustration.

experiences altogether. This decision is often triggered by occurrences where one or more story elements do not work such as bad acting, bad writing, substandard special effects, technology not working or the overall loss of believability. Once that happens, the whole story structure can come crashing down, especially if the core story itself is not strong enough to balance out any weaknesses in the supporting elements; after all, there are amazing stories from days past still relevant with outdated effects. Furthermore, with many well-established channels for voicing opinion, those who feel let down will not turn their back in silence, but vent their frustration via channels like social media, influencing the opinion of others.

RELEVANCY, RELATABILITY AND BELIEVABILITY

For the audience to give in and let go, certain critical elements of the story need to work and work well. Very well, actually. There are many, many brilliant books written on the matter of narrative structures and what makes a story stand out to the point of being great art. However, when looking specifically at the moment when the story and the audience make contact as part of a designed relationship between the two, a series of universal and monumental guidelines for creating and maintaining a connection towards the point of suspension and disbelief and immersion can be defined.

Is your story matter relevant?

The story needs to be relevant to the audience, not just in an overall way, such as general issues most people will agree on by default, but on a personal level. This relevancy has to be evident even before the audience buys the book, the ticket or the game; they are most likely not to spend their time and money simply to figure out if something is relevant or interesting to them. Which is why marketing spending, free book chapters and game demos are justifiable to advance the state of opinion by the audience from awareness to interest to the desire to wanting to experience more of what is offered to them.

> Relevancy on a personal level is so impactful because, at its core, every great story is about us and who we are.

Relevancy on a personal level is so impactful because, at its core, every great story is about us and who we are. Heroes, villains and sidekicks alike are relatable to the audience because they mirror themselves and their everyday lives in even the most extraordinary situations that the story characters find themselves in. When the protagonist is struggling to understand an alien world or an alien envoy, it represents a reflection of the struggle to understand the real world around us, our place in it, and the hardships of communication and connections between people. Even within an alien setting, the frustration presented to the audience is understandable and relatable.

Furthermore, when presented through relatable characters, the extraordinary scenarios the audience witness, makes the audience ask themselves, more or less knowingly, what they would actually do if facing the same situation, while still allowing themselves to let loose and feel the rush of the hero, knowing that in real life, they may turn and run away.

Are your characters relatable?

Regardless of media and format, the audience needs characters they can relate to. Characters without depth or the capability of invoking emotion will make the story superficial and unrelatable, which arguably occurs when feature films tip the balance towards special effects over character and story development. If the spectacle in itself cannot attract and maintain the interest of the moviegoer, the film becomes an empty vehicle for showcasing the latest CGI[5] and other visual fireworks. Eye candy that does not have the same longevity as a relatable person's victory or defeat.

The relation with the character is built on emotions that trigger the empathy, sympathy, likes and dislikes of the character. The most intriguing and believable characters have more nuances, which allows the hero to have her or his doubts. In the Star Wars franchise, Luke Skywalker is often in doubt of which path to follow. The interesting villains did not choose to be evil for evil's sake but have an agenda or a cause they consider the right path to follow. In another Star Wars reference, many of those fighting in the ranks of the Galactic Empire are convinced they do what they need to do to bring order to a chaotic and lawless galaxy. Finally, it is believable, although surprising, when the sidekick does heroic acts even to the point of becoming a martyr. Within the Star Wars universe, R2-D2 and C3PO have had their moments as both comic reliefs and saviours of the day, although sometimes by accident.

On an important side note, relatability also depends on the audience knowing the references they are presented with. Consider the Star Wars franchise used for the examples above. If you have no knowledge of the franchise, some of the above may be confusing or hard to relate to. However, if you are told that Luke Skywalker is a farm boy in a galaxy far, far away that is hesitant in joining the rebellion against the ruling evil Galactic Empire, but when he finally does, he becomes a key person in overthrowing it, aided by his friends such as the droids – androids – C3PO and R2-D2, a different reference and meaning is established. This is a very basic example as to why creators need to consider the existing or lacking relation to pre-existing content. In other words, what the Audience Programming is, one of the design principles of Integrated Storytelling introduced previously in this book.

Is your storyworld believable?

The events endured by the characters should be framed by a believable storyworld, one that is a credible and relatable environment for the story to take place. To get to this point, elaborate worldbuilding[6] may be required, during which much more than a map of an imaginative region is created. It is the combined design of geography, environments, nature, wildlife, habitats, inhabitants, social structures, nations, cultures, allies and enemies, and so on and so forth; everything that is needed to present the audience with a rich setting. This world plays into the backstory and the characteristics of those living in it. Creatures and characters may look and act differently, whether they are in a harsh desert environment or in a green, lush environment. The world have a deeper purpose than being just a backdrop to the character's actions. It Enhances the mood and the emotion of the story, chapters, scenes and those who dwell here. Living in a dark, underground cave surrounded by lava and glowing eyes builds a certain kind of character for heroes and villains alike.

The audience will not always be consciously aware of every detail of a storyworld, but its elaborateness ensures consistency and conscious or subconscious appreciation of depth.

The audience will not always be consciously aware of every detail of a storyworld, but its elaborateness ensures consistency and conscious or subconscious appreciation of depth.

In addition, even the most outlandish places will usually reflect structures and logics the audience already knows, such a social structure with lands, borders, leadership and citizenship, to avoid having to explain a whole new kind of social structure. To enhance the feeling of being alien without alienating the audience, these structures are sometimes taken from existing non-human species or are an exaggeration of a culture different from what the creator represents. The xenomorphs from the Alien franchise are parasitic insects living in hives born from a xenomorph queen. The depiction of enemies in Western pop culture reflects those who are perceived as adversaries in real life at the time; Native Americans, Nazis, Soviets, Arabs and Russians are among those groups who have been representative of the villain in a direct or interpreted form. The antagonists may not be explicitly presented or mentioned as being one of the above but is undoubtedly reminiscent of them.

The characters and the world – or worlds – they inhabit are connected by a narrative structure. The structure draws in and retains the audience with a combination of events bringing the protagonist further to or from her or his goal, uncovering new insight in mysteries and backstories while developing characters through not only what we are told about them, but also through our observations of their actions and behaviour. This narrative structure contains the story elements to the audience at carefully selected points in time; they become moments that in sequence make up the overall story experience. The storyline becomes more than the journey of the characters, as it is shared with an engaged and immersed audience who walk beside them. A journey that becomes even richer and more immersive when integrating, combining and balancing the established concepts of storytelling and experience design.

DEFINING STORYTELLING

Storytelling has the power and capability to create connections between people, places, products, messages and causes, and a new breed of storytellers is embracing its impact, whether they are an upcoming generation of aspiring professionals, start-ups or an established organisation. With the increased recognition of storytelling, there are grounds for confusion, misunderstandings and hype.

Storytelling is the next big thing, but what exactly storytelling is. There is no simple answer and adding to the confusion what is perceived as storytelling by one may not be so by the other, and the age-old discipline is continuously branching out. Still, if one goes looking for them, the short definitions are to be found in various places, some relevant examples include:

> *Storytelling is the conveying of events in words, and images, often by improvisation or embellishment. Stories or narratives have been shared in every culture as a means of entertainment, education, cultural preservation, and to instil moral values. Crucial elements of stories and storytelling include plot, characters, and narrative point of view.*[7]
> *(Storytelling is) the act and skills of presenting stories and tales.*[8]

In an interesting statement by the National Storytelling Network,[9] storytelling was defined by having an interactive element to it, the interaction not being defined as digital, but as two-way interaction between the storyteller and the audience. This is interesting in relation to Integrated Storytelling because it expands the concept of storytelling to include the influence of the audience on the storytelling process:

> *Storytelling is the interactive art of using words and actions to reveal the elements and images of a story while encouraging the listener's imagination.*[10]

The definitions of storytelling and the discussion about these definitions is an ongoing process, as the relevancy and impact of storytelling on culture and community and vice versa are in a continuous state of flux. Not at least because of the accelerated evolution and adaption of digital media by the mainstream audience. However, for a definition in the context of this book, storytelling will be defined as follows:

> Storytelling is the art of presenting, engaging and moving the audience with fully structured narratives presenting well-developed plot and characters.

It is possible to add specific considerations to this overall definition:

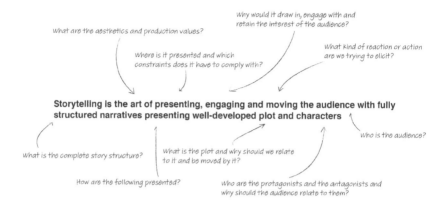

Why would it draw in, engage with and retain the interest of the audience?

What are the aesthetics and production values?

Where is it presented and which constraints does it have to comply with?

What kind of reaction or action are we trying to elicit?

Storytelling is the art of presenting, engaging and moving the audience with fully structured narratives presenting well-developed plot and characters

What is the complete story structure?

What is the plot and why should we relate to it and be moved by it?

Who is the audience?

How are the following presented?

Who are the protagonists and the antagonists and why should the audience relate to them?

These specific questions are not a linear or even complete list of decisions made one time only, but a series of interrelated and mutually influential considerations that the story creator will circle back to again and again while developing the story and how it is to be brought to life.

DEFINING EXPERIENCES

> Creative experience design is the art and craft of constructing memories that last.

Creative experience design is the art and craft of constructing memories that last. They are made up from a combination of moments and events that are communicated to our brains via sensory inputs and are subsequently either forgotten or embedded as memories. As they occur, they release different kinds of natural physical chemicals in reaction to what the audience see, hear, feel taste or smell with either of their five senses. Their imprint can be made in both what can be defined as psychological and as physical memory, and even as experiences are often considered intangible, their memory can outlast the lifetime of many tangible, physical objects.

A psychological, or cognitive, memory can be the imprint something one is told or presented with as a story in a book, in an exciting talk or an eye-opening documentary. Physical memories do not necessarily require the cognitive recall of specific details when used for driving a car or a bike, or when remembering the taste of a favourite meal or the sound of a favourite melody. We remember with our senses. The physical memories are, so to speak, embedded in the body, where the psychological memory could be said to be embedded in the mind. This is for argument's sake, of course, as all of it is actually stored as impulses in our brains, whether consciously or not.

A simple description of physical memory

Combining the five senses can have a compelling impact on the perception of an event. When you are reading this book, you may sip a nice cup of coffee, listen to music or try not to be disturbed by anyone. Trained lecturers are aware that students learn in different combinations of sensory perception. Some students are more attuned to sound, so they get very distracted by ambient noise or the clicking of a pen during a presentation. For others, taking notes is a way to create a sensory imprint in order to recall the material they are presented with. It can be argued that sensory inputs are always combined in some way. Even when reading a book in a closed room, the chair, the cup of coffee, the light and a draft of the window all becomes part of the audience story experience. Sensory design as a means for creating lasting memories is widespread and powerful.

Off the record, representatives from a well-established theme park brand once shared that they had found that the recall of details from a specific place increased 300% if they planted roses on designated visitor photo-op locations, utilising the powerful sense of smell.

A simple description of psychological memory

The psyche also holds the power to trigger emotion through a chemical or electrical effect in the brain. It can be the cognitive response to a murder mystery, or the emotional response to sadness, joy or fear invoked by tragedy, comedy and horror respectively, or even the release of endorphins in the brains of the audience from watching an action sequence, even though one is just watching them on a screen. It has even been argued that the negative aspect of this release of 'pseudo-endorphins' is that it can act as a substitute for real-life experiences, keeping people away from experiencing reality and creating their own, unique memories in a real-world setting.[11]

However, as the virtual environments explored in a game is widely considered the endeavours of the gamer. Considering experiences on the screen or in a virtual environment as being pseudo or lesser experiences needs to be evaluated and taking into more nuanced consideration. Adding to the point; if you can win considerable cash prizes in e-sports, how does the argument real versus unreal hold up based on whether the action occurs on the physical or the virtual realm?

How does the argument real versus unreal hold up based on whether the action occurs on the physical or the virtual realm?

Good and great experiences are not defined by whether they are funny, comfortable or the opposite.

They are determined by the depth and longevity of impression they leave through the combination of sensory and cognitive inputs. Riding a roller coaster or going to the gym is not comfortable all the time but elicits a positive and energised condition in their aftermaths. On a less interactive scale, the same applies to books, movies and television; they may not be comfortable to read or watch but can still entertain or enlighten. Finishing a book can add a sense of accomplishment.

The positive impact of people activating their body or mind, challenging mindsets and releasing endorphins will stay with them. Going beyond choosing one or either, the combination of body and mind makes for the creation of more profound and longer-lasting memories; what is experienced has a combined higher recall on multiple levels. Sometimes, being immersed in an experience will be so powerful that it even acts as a transformative experience: when the audience takes on the role of the hero in an imagined reality, they may have somehow changed perceptions when they return. Back in the real world, their new mindset may lead to action.

Interfacing with the experience

Experience design is sometimes used as a terminology for what is basically the user experience when using a screen of a device, or some other form pushing buttons and completing computerised tasks.

However, that is a limited perception, even as interaction design by now have widely adapted the values of aesthetics as an integral part. Experience design predates digital media as a way of building a platform where the audience can interact and interface with elements of a story. It has been a discipline for designing themed spaces for the better part of a century; one that has always evolved with, and pushed, the advancements of technology. When audiences interface with these experiences, moments are created and transformed into memory by combining elements of both function and emotion. The connection with and the context of the experience can take on a multitude of forms.

> It can be argued that you can never fully design an experience.

It can be argued that you can never fully design an experience, as the final memory to a high degree is influenced by human interaction and reaction. According to this mindset, experience design is about creating the framework for great experiences, not trying to define them in every detail or function. As is the case with storytelling, one can never truly control every single aspect of the individual experience. Every memory will have some shared elements, but will ultimately be unique, something that we see explored increasingly in attractions, games and interactive stories.

Acknowledging experience as memories being purposely created and kept in the minds and hearts of the audience through physical and psychological inputs, our definition in the context of this book is as follows:

> Experiences are events that become memorable moments through the balanced, combined power of sensory and cognitive inputs.

This definition can be elaborated into specific considerations to further the design and creation of experiences:

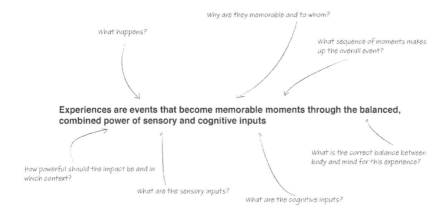

As the definition for storytelling above, this is not a linear or formulaic way of making experiences, but a circular model to be revisited again and again, as the experience in development evolves from idea to a concept and a design.

DEFINING INTEGRATED

The concepts of storytelling and experience have been explored and defined above, as mentioned, in the context of this book. The overall context of it is the integration multiple disciplines into a new hybrid of storytelling and experience that is based on the balance and the full potential of the two in combination: Integrated Storytelling. It allows for applying while transcending current technology, redefine the relationship between story, creator and audience and provides a wide range of possible ways of implementation and integration. At its core, Integrated Storytelling is the new dynamic of the story influencing the audience, and the

> At its core, Integrated Storytelling is the new dynamic of the story influencing the audience, and the audience influencing the story.

audience influencing the story. In order to make this happen, a shifting role of the creator is called for, one that includes being the integrator or ensuring that integration happens, in order to avoid fragmentation and confusion.

Not unlike storytelling and experience, the term integrated has multiple meanings in multiple contexts and is often used in the description of various disciplines, such as Integrated Marketing and Integrated Systems.

Integrated Marketing is marketing efforts that combine and works across media (cross-media), multiple channels (omnichannel) and customer touchpoints. It ultimately integrates efforts across different divisions such as marketing, product development and service to reach and engage with customers at every life cycle of product development, purchase and post-sale experience. An organisation that applies Integrated Marketing to its full extent goes beyond Integrated Marketing Communications (IMC) and work to break down departmental and disciplinary silos.

Integrated Systems are a combination of different IT systems or applications that are merged to deliver that which the stand-alone systems were not capable of on their own. This does not just include IT back-end oddities, but also front-end design, and the adaption and integration of a start-up app company with an established major platform. Sometimes, the integrated systems will co-exist, sometimes they will become something new, and sometimes, as is often the case with more prominent companies buying smaller ones, the technology of the latter will be assimilated to become features in the bigger platform. The latter scenario is arguable not integration but assimilation. For any Trekkies reading this,[12] think the Federation versus the Borg empire; be with us versus become us.

When researching integration as the combination of different elements rather than the mere assimilation of one by the other, one can find different examples of definitions of the word, including but far from limited to:

> *Two or more things combined in order to become more effective.*[13]
> *Combining or coordinating separate elements so as to provide a harmonious, interrelated whole.*[14]

With the keywords being combination and a harmonious, interrelated whole, concerning Integrated Storytelling, integration in this book is defined as follows:

> Integration is the combination of story experiences that can exist on their own, but in co-existence become a harmonious, interrelated whole that builds and evolves through every encounter the audience has with the integrated story universe.

Similar to Storytelling and Experiences, the definition can be elaborated with specific considerations:

How are they combined?

What are the story experiences and what are their relations?

To what extent and where?

Integration is the combination of story experiences that can exist on their own, but in co-existence become a harmonious, interrelated whole that builds and evolves through every encounter the audience has with the integrated story universe.

What are the dimensions of integration?

Who is the audience?

What is the story universe that contains the stories?

What are the connection points, interface and influence linking the story to the audience?

How do they interrelate and influence each other to become more than the sum of their parts?

How do more story experiences become more than the sum of their parts?

Once again, these questions are not to be understood as a linear list of one-time decisions but are considerations that the story creator will revisit again and again in various cycles of development, design and updates as more content and features are added to the Integrated Storytelling experience once launched.

STORY DESIGN THINKING

To combine story and experience into an integrated story experience, it is necessary to add a new level to the various and valuable storytelling methods that are being applied to books, films, television, etc., as well as the experiential disciplines such as game design methods applied for video games and interactive adventures. This new level needs to relate to experience and story simultaneously while combining either as an integral part allowing for multiple levels of audience influence and interaction. The story structure needs to become a design structure.

Enter design thinking

The concept of Design Thinking was made popular by Tim Brook of the internationally renowned design studio IDEO in the book *Change by Design: How Design Thinking Transforms Organizations and Inspires Innovation*,[15] as a method for driving organisational innovation forward.

Design Thinking in its essence is design as a process, not as a design output.

Design Thinking, in its essence, is design as a process, not as a design output, be it visual, multimedia, products or other, and makes the process of 'to design' take precedence over delivering 'a design'. Design Thinking allows for exploring different possibilities in an overlap of inspiration, ideation and implementation while ensuring not getting stuck in a perpetual discussion by applying constraints of design processes as a project that has a defined beginning, middle and end.

Applied to the development of story experiences, the exploring of possibilities and the testing of possible scenarios is essential to determine which aspects of a story experience design to prioritise, framed by constraints such as space, experience length, budget and with a set deadline for preproduction or production to begin. By applying Design Thinking early in the process, the best foundation can be set for utilising multiple disciplines simultaneously, as is needed when wanting to integrate story and experience into something new without being overwhelmed with the vastness of possible combinations. Design Thinking helps forward experimentation as well as simplification, because each step of a design process helps focus and prioritise the elements of an Integrated Storytelling structure. It can help create the story and the experience before a single word is written in the script.

From storyteller to story designer

The combination of story and experience is at the brink of the emergence of a new story creation industry that will thrive through the application of design at depth in a new industry landscape, where storytelling will evolve from its current state towards new iterations and manifestations. The steps of this evolution of the story experience and those who create, or aspire to create them, may very well follow steps similar to those taken by other organisations adapting to Design Thinking. For the creator, these steps are the path of transformation from storyteller to story designer, regardless of whether the creator in question is a person or a company.

Non-design: Story creation that does not use design systematically.

Design as styling: Design is used purely for styling and presentation of stories, often as production design or production value.

Design as an innovation process: Design is an integral part of innovating new story experiences.

Design as a creative strategy: Design is an integral part of the story designer's creative strategy for story experience design and creation.

Design as organisation: Design plays a part in the organisational structure of individual and teams that rethink and reinvent roles and forms of collaboration to provide audience-oriented story experiences.

Individuals and organisations aspiring to create a position as story designers need to consider what step they are currently at, and what kind of initiatives and projects will set the direction for a future positioning. In doing so, it is crucial to keep and maintain a Design Thinking mindset with the audience at the centre of the design. A future role or position is not reached by always putting brand, story or

> In Story Design Thinking, the audience takes precedence. They are the heroes at the centre of the universe.

experience considerations first. In Story Design Thinking, the audience takes precedence. They are the heroes at the centre of the universe and should be considered as such in everything related to the conceptualisation, design and creation of story experiences. When invited into the storyworlds that are created, they become lead characters, stars and heroes of the events that unfolds around them.

DEFINING INTEGRATED STORYTELLING

A short and concise definition for Integrated Storytelling can be created through the merging the definitions already established for Storytelling, Experiences and Integration in this chapter.

> Integrated Storytelling is an audience-centric, multi-dimensional story experience design that applies, combines and transcends disciplines and technologies to create sustainable concepts that build and grow through every encounter with their audiences.

This definition can also have specific considerations added for conceptualisation, design and creation:

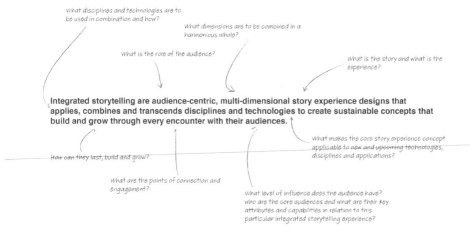

What disciplines and technologies are to be used in combination and how?

What dimensions are to be combined in a harmonious whole?

What is the role of the audience?

What is the story and what is the experience?

Integrated storytelling are audience-centric, multi-dimensional story experience designs that applies, combines and transcends disciplines and technologies to create sustainable concepts that build and grow through every encounter with their audiences.

What makes the core story experience concept applicable to new and upcoming technologies, disciplines and applications?

How can they last, build and grow?

What are the points of connection and engagement?

What level of influence does the audience have? who are the core audiences and what are their key attributes and capabilities in relation to this particular integrated storytelling experience?

As with the other definitions, the Integrated Storytelling definition and its specific points are not a step-by-step rule book. It is a sequence of considerations to be continuously revisited as part of the design and development of an Integrated Storytelling design in order to build a concept core that is as strong and sustainable as possible.

NOTES

1. IP: Intellectual Property
2. Dark ride: A ride that is placed inside, such as haunted houses, only lit by artificial lighting
3. https://www.walibi.be/en/attractions/popcorn-revenge
4. Rockstar Games: Red Dead Redemption 2 (2018)
5. CGI: Computer-Generated Imagery
6. Worldbuilding is the process of constructing an imaginary world
7. https://www.definitions.net/definition/storytelling
8. https://www.definitions.net/definition/storytelling
9. https://storynet.org/
10. https://storynet.org/what-is-storytelling
11. Rients Riskes: Endorfiner (2001)
12. Trekkies: devoted fans of the Star Trek franchise.
13. https://dictionary.cambridge.org/dictionary/english/integrated
14. https://www.merriam-webster.com/dictionary/integrated
15. Tim Brook: Change by Design: How Design Thinking Transforms Organizations (2019)

CHAPTER 7

The War of the Worlds

TRANSCENDING CONTEMPORARY TECHNOLOGY FROM NINETEENTH CENTURY BOOK TO TWENTY-FIRST CENTURY IMMERSIVE EXPERIENCE

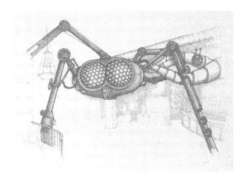

Sketch of Martian Fighting Machine for The Spirit of Man Bar & Restaurant at Jeff Wayne's The War of The Worlds: The Immersive Experience.

The War of the Worlds started as written words in its initial format of a book by H.G. Wells, which has proven to be a concept that is capable of using and transcending contemporary technologies from the 1800s through the 1900s and well into the twenty-first century. Furthermore, the concept of the malevolent alien invaders has proven to be strong enough to have made an impact well beyond literature and popular culture, from allegedly causing panic as a radio show[1] to ultimately shape the perception of what a hostile invasion by hostile, technological advanced aliens would be like.

The concept of the malevolent alien invaders has proven to be strong enough to have made an impact well beyond literature and popular culture.

English writer H.G. Wells made his mark in the late-nineteenth century and early-twentieth century, combining his insight in sciences and philosophy to create some of the most influential science-fiction literature of all time. At its core, the science-fiction genre can be described as the stories that are based on the question 'what if…', with mechanics driven by science and the advancements it provides. 'What if we could travel to the stars?', 'What if robots became sentient beings?', 'What if we could travel through time?', 'What if we go into space and find that we are not alone?' or, perhaps even more frightening, 'What if we venture into space and find that we are alone?' These are just some of the questions that have been the basis of many a good story, based on or made plausible by scientific advancements.

FROM JOURNEYS OF WONDER
TO CAUTIONARY TALES

H.G. Wells asked some of these questions in some of the most prominent books from his rich bibliography of half a century of literary work, including 'The Time Machine' (where Wells coined the descriptive phrase time traveller) (1895), 'The Invisible Man' (1897), 'The Island of Doctor Moreau' and 'The War of the Worlds' (1898).

Each of them is among the defining milestones in the science-fiction genre. They also mark a departure from the fantastic voyages of the French author Jules Verne, author of such pivotal, meticulously researched yet somewhat light-hearted books as 'Twenty Thousand Leagues Under the Seas: A Tour of the Underwater World' (1870), 'Around the World in Eighty Days' (1875) and 'Journey to the Center of the Earth' (1864). H.G. Wells's work carved another path for the genre than the celebration of the wondrous possibilities brought forward by science; his work can fittingly be described as tales of caution.

The two paths laid down by Verne and Wells respectively influence any work of science fiction to this day, regardless of form of delivery or media; the possibilities, the journey into the unknown and the cautionary tale. Consider the difference of the murderous time-travelling Terminators from a dystopian future versus the loveable droids in Star Wars, taking part in adventures across fantastical worlds in a space opera set in a galaxy far, far away.

The great, everlasting tales of science fiction are concerned about more than exploring possibilities brought forward by technical advancements;

they are about those who are affected by the events that ensues and are more often than not about our humanity and society, rather than merely stargazing wonders. The mirror science fiction holds up in front of us reflects and comments on our existing reality while asking questions of what we as individuals, society and humanity, in general, would do in the 'What if...' scenarios. As stated by Will Storr in *'The Science of Storytelling'*,[2] great stories need to be relevant on a personal level and make us question what the audience would do in any given situation they are presented with. Would they become heroes? Indifferent bystanders? Perhaps even villains?

While some science-fiction stories provide mere escapism at first glance, many are reflective on today's society, more or less calling for awareness or action from the audience. It is no coincidence that Margaret Atwood's dystopian masterpiece *The Handmaids Tale*[3] became one of the most notable books, then movie, then the award-winning television series that premiered at the time of a rise of the very issues, it criticised. Even the most outlandish of tales are made relevant through their references to the real world we live in, and because of this, have the potential to live on as lasting concepts, as long as the issues they portray persist.

> Even the most outlandish of tales are made relevant through their references to the real world we live in.

DEFINING THE ALIEN INVASION

With *The War of the Worlds*, H.G. Wells provided the very foundation for the modern alien invasion concept, one that would have a long-lasting impact across media, fiction and even science, and have stayed relevant for well over a decade. The story had become a cross-media[4] franchise before either of the words was related to media or storytelling.

The simplified premise of *The War of the Worlds* begins with the Martians, having watched Earth with envy, deciding to invade the planet and eradicate its human population in order to rule it. Once the Martian invasion fleet comes to Earth, their very first contact is violent; they crash into the ground, penetrating it violently, rather than the almost serene hovering we have seen from other alien spacecraft. When people approach the alien ships, still hopeful that the visitors come in peace, the Martians reveal themselves as octopus-like alien beings (note that once again, even the most alien of species have some sort of recognisable features), and within moments, start killing everyone in sight with death rays. A scenario that has been mimicked with more or less variations on many occasions in other representations of alien invasion in movies, books, games and so on – and arguably one that has helped build a shared fear of aliens not paying friendly visits as in Spielberg's *Close Encounters of the Third Kind* (1977) or *E.T. The Extra-Terrestrial* (1982) but to destroy the world as we know it.

The humans fight back, but to no avail, and the chances for survival for the original inhabitants of Earth grows dim as the aliens unleash their war machines, the tripods. They are giant three-legged mechanical constructions carrying death rays that with their tentacles and menacing alien calling signal almost become like alien creatures themselves. The battle of Earth rages on, and even as the humans have a few wins, the war is lost.

One of the distinctions of *The War of The Worlds* is the role of the main character. Not the hero to bring down the alien invaders, he is instead tossed around by events beyond his control, observing first-hand how the invasion becomes war and borders on defeat. His primary concern and mission become to survive and be united with his loved one. As such, his journey becomes a very realistic portrayal of how most would act when they find themselves in a war zone. The first perspective is not that of a hero, but a refugee fleeing an advancing and advanced enemy, which makes the story immensely relevant to this day. He witnesses many of the events unfolding first-hand, and even meets a person with a grandiose plan to abandon the surface, leave it to the Martians and go deep underground to build a 'brave new world'. A possible future where the fate of humankind is to stay below ground to survive, one that is revisited a century later in the Matrix (1999; –2021) franchise, where the world is not overtaken by aliens, but by machines.

Just as it seems like all is lost, and the world itself is beginning to look alien, being covered in red weed, the tripods grind to a halt. It soon becomes evident that the Martians have succumbed to an unexpected ally, that is, bacteria that have proved fatal to the alien invaders, effectively killing them all. In the end, the war is not won by humans, but by the smallest of creatures on our planet; a lesson in humility for aliens and humans alike.

THE DEEPER RELEVANCE, THEN AND NOW

There are both obvious and subtle commentary and reflection on the late-nineteenth century in *The War of the Worlds*, making it a tale much deeper than the event of an invasion from outer space and adding to it the longevity that keeps it exciting and relevant today. The alien invasion can be viewed as a commentary on colonialism, and how history would unfold if the tables were turned on The British Empire, with it becoming the conquered or colonised by a superior, more advanced force. The tripods can be seen as being representative of the negative impact and fear for the industrialism and dehumanisation of work, similar to the ongoing discussion about and concern for technology and Artificial Intelligence (AI) taking over the roles of human labour, and possibly, the world. Furthermore, the cautionary tale describes how all-out war with no concerns for civilian lives turns the battleground into an outer-worldly wasteland, an eerie premonition of the two world wars that would follow, the first one only 16 years later.

The storyline of the main characters describing how they are diminished from being members of a thriving society to refugees seeking a safe haven is as relevant as ever. In the setting of *The War of The Worlds*, acts of heroism and cowardice happen in parallel, but in the larger scheme of things, they do not really make a difference, a fear that is being shared by many; not being in control of their lives, not being able to influence their fate. The world is not saved by humankind; it is saved by bacteria, which essentially means that the Earth and its flora and fauna hold power to save man, who in turn choose to push nature and wildlife to the point of extinction. *The War of the Worlds* is far from today's formulaic blockbuster with its protagonist not being the hero, and in leaving the audience with the knowledge that there most likely are more Martians left on their home world. Martians that, given their adverse nature would most likely regroup, assess their loses and learnings, and prepare for another strike. Still, the original story ends here.

> Acts of heroism and cowardice happen in parallel, but in the larger scheme of things, they do not really make a difference.

THE EVOLUTIONARY MEDIA TIMELINE OF THE WAR OF THE WORLDS

The evolution and the continued presence and relevance of *The War of The Worlds* have tied in with the evolution of media, giving the story new platforms and new ways of being experienced. The concept is a fascinating example of a strong story that has proven itself capable of transcending current media and technology to the point of influencing perceptions of possible realities and alien life. It is worth mentioning, though, that alien life may be so different from ours

> The concept is a fascinating example of a strong story that has proven itself capable of transcending current media and technology.

that they may be beyond the concept of offensive invasion. The timeline of selected vital points of *The War of the Worlds* story experience can be listed and put into perspective related to the evolution of media and history at large.

1830s: Marks the 70th year of the industrial revolution and the full impact of it on Britain.

1898: *The War of the Worlds* is published as a book.

1914–1918: World War I.

1920s: Radio is broadcast to a national audience in the United States.

1938: *The War of the Worlds* is broadcast in a newscast format by Orson Welles. As the story goes, causing panic among listeners, who thinks the invasion is real.

1939–1945: World War II.

1947: The Cold War begins.

1947: Kenneth Arnold U.F.O. sighting that sparked the name flying saucers. The sighting is considered the start of the modern U.F.O. era.

1947: The Roswell incident where United States Army Air Forces allegedly captured a crashed flying saucer.

1953: *The War of the Worlds* is released as a feature film starring Gene Barry and Barré Lyndon and narrated by Sir Cedric Hardwicke. The setting is changed from late–eighth century England to 1953 California. The tripods are presented as flying aircraft more akin to the flying saucers made popular in 1950s U.F.O. folklore.

1954: *The War of the Worlds* is published as a comic book adaption in the Classics Illustrated series.

1956: The Golden Age of comic book ends and the Silver Age begins, where comic books become a mainstream source of entertainment in America.

1967: John Christopher publishes *The Tripods Trilogy*, a series of books for children ages 9 and older, that can be read as a vision of what would happen if the Martians took over the Earth without destroying it and rather than annihilating the population, making it their willing subjects.

1977: Atari is released.

1978: Jeff Wayne's *Musical Version of The War of the Worlds* is released as an album.

1982: *War of the Worlds* is released as a monochrome vector arcade game.

1983: Nintendo is released.

1988: *War of the Worlds* television series continues the original story decades after the original story.

1989: Tim Berners-Lee invents the World Wide Web and creates the first web browser in 1990.

1991: The Cold War ends.

1991: Sega is released.

1993: Mosaic, later renamed Netscape, was launched as the first graphical internet browser, and popularised the World Wide Web and the internet among a mass audience.

1994: PlayStation is released.

1998: Jeff Wayne's *The War of the Worlds* is released as a video game.

2001: Xbox is released.

2005: *War of the Worlds*, Stephen Spielberg's feature film version is released, starring Tom Cruise set in the modern-day United States.

2006: Graphic novel version of the original story by writer Ben Edginton and artist D'Israeli is published by Dark Horse Comics.

2006: Jeff Wayne's *Musical Version of The War of The Worlds* is brought to the stage for the first time, playing to sold-out arenas across the United Kingdom. *The War of The Worlds Live* is a spectacular mix of live music, theatre, multi-media and visual arts on a grand scale.

2005: *War of the Worlds* is redone as a full-length movie for video release.

2007: iPhone launches.

2007: Netflix starts streaming video content online.

2008: *War of the Worlds 2: The Next Wave* is released as a full-length sequel to the 2005 movie.

2010: iPad launches.

The Spirit of Man Bar & Restaurant at Jeff Wayne's The War of The Worlds: The Immersive Experience.

2011: *The War of the Worlds* launches as a console game, with the story set in 1950s London.

2012: *War of the Worlds: Goliath* is released as a full-length animated feature as a steampunk sequel to the original story.

2016: Oculus Rift is released, marking a new era of V.R. experiences.

2019: *The War of the Worlds* T.V. mini-series is released by B.B.C., with the storyline being set in the Edwardian Era (1901–1910).

2019: The War of the Worlds Immersive Experience opens in London. Working as a team, visitors must survive the Martian attack as they smell, touch and feel their way around 25 themed areas over 22,000 square feet.

The variations above of the story and the platforms where it is represented, is hardly complete. It does, however, show how the concept of the *War of the Worlds* has evolved across time, platforms and history in its various formats as books, comic books, radio shows, movies, television series, musical, games and, in 2019, an immersive show that brings the audience into the world of the storyline.

The War of the Worlds Immersive Experience makes perfect use of nonlinear storytelling, interaction, transmedia, technology and live action in what can be described as a prime example of the harmonious whole that is Integrated Storytelling at its best.

The book that was written in the shadow of the smoking furnaces of the industrial revolution lives on as a concept that continues to apply current and future technology in a multitude of innovative ways.

NOTES

1. Orson Welles: The War of the Worlds Radio Drama (1938)
2. Will Storr: The Science of Storytelling (2020)
3. Margaret Atwood: The Handmaid's Tale (1985)
4. Cross-media: The distribution of content amongst different media

CHAPTER 8

CASE: Jeff Wayne's The War of The Worlds: The Immersive Experience

Jeff Wayne's The War of The Worlds: The Immersive Experience combines music, immersive theatre, virtual reality, augmented reality, holograms and other cutting-edge technology to give audiences the chance to live through the Martian invasion of 1898.

Visitors will be thrust into the heart of the story from the moment they step inside the vast 22,000-square foot multi-level site in Central London, which has been transformed for the unique Martian adventure.[1]

The narrative of the experience was written to follow the H.G. Wells book faithfully as well as Wayne's album, and it invites the audience to become part of the storyverse and visit its places and experience the events

Official Artwork for Jeff Wayne's The War of The Worlds: The Immersive Experience.

described within first hand. In the experience, the audience becomes a citizen that is trying to escape the Martians with the setup being that they follow 'The Journalist', George and his wife Carrie who recount the 1898 invasion, which happened several years prior.

The experience follows a linear storyline and is split into two acts that in total take around 110 minutes, including a 20-minute intermission halfway through. Audiences share the experience in a group of up to 12 people. They are led to a variety of environments either with the help of VR headsets or actual actors in detailed Victorian costumes. In the VR experience parts, audiences get a virtual body looking like a Victorian character themselves, chosen from a range of different characters at random. Through their VR sets, the participants can see each other's character, adapting the experience to the number of people who are in it.

Jeff Wayne's The War of The Worlds: The Immersive Experience is created to immerse the audience into the universe created by H.G. Wells and Jeff Wayne, with the help of many kinds of new and innovative technologies. It wants to induce feelings of fear and wonder, creating both a scary and magical experience as audiences find themselves escaping the Martians that have invaded Earth. The audience is immersed further by engaging all their senses, smell, feel, sight, sound and even taste before, during and after the show. This brings them as close to experiencing the events of the story as possible.

VR headset footage from Jeff Wayne's The War of The Worlds: The Immersive Experience.

The high-quality performances of the real-life actors make the scenes and story believable and engage the visitors as they are guided through the narrative. Using actual, living people to guide audiences and tell their story alongside all the technologies creates a multi-layered experience that may help blur the line between the digital and the virtual world.

The experience was inspired by phantasmagoria shows – a form of horror theatre from the Victorian era – utilising the same techniques but updating them with modern technologies. The combination of using different cutting-edge technologies to further a narrative and create an audience-centric experience makes this experience an innovative, award-winning show.[2]

The use of holograms, 360-degree projection mapping, VR, AR and real actors with the goal of immersing the visitor makes The War of the Worlds The Immersive Experience a unique and a prime example of interdisciplinary story experience design.

Location: London, UK
Created by theatre company Dotdotdot
Opened for the public on 31 May 2019
Area: 22,000 sq. ft.
Experience: Includes 24 scenes
The experience combines immersive theatre, virtual reality, augmented reality, holograms and cutting-edge technology.
Duration: Around 2 hours including a 20-minute intermission in the Red Weed Bar.
In 2020, it won a TEA Thea Award for Outstanding Achievement in the category of Connected Immersion.
Jeff Wayne is an award-winning composer. His musical interpretation of H.G. Wells's **'The War of The Worlds'** released in 1978 won two UK 'Ivor Novello' Awards and the USA's 'Best Recording in Science Fiction and Fantasy'.

NOTES

1. https://www.dotdot.london/the-experience" insert https://thewaroftheworldsimmersive.com/the-experience/
2. https://www.avinteractive.com/features/case-studies/war-worlds-immersive-take- classic-tale-15-07-2019

CHAPTER 9

From theory to practice: Concepts transcending technologies

H.G. Wells's *The War of the Worlds* is of course not the only concept that was originally presented in one format to move on to other ways of being experienced. There are a multitude of ideas and narratives that have been successfully established across various disciplines and platforms.

However, there are also those that one would have thought would succeed but did not manage to do so. There can be various reasons for the latter.

Perhaps, the copyright holder or franchise owner did not accept to work with others in bringing the creative work to other formats and did not have the capability to do this successfully without assistance.

Perhaps, the first step from the original format to another did not succeed in gaining the appeal from a wider audience, sometimes due to inferior production, acting, etc., and any motivation to move forward across multiple platforms was effectively terminated. In order for a concept to transcend current technologies, which first step from one platform to another, is as crucial as it is to define what is the concept actually is, once the media or platform is stripped away.

Going from theory to practice, the following experiment can help identify and engineer a story from one platform to the next. To begin, it is necessary to take a step backward first.

- Choose a storyline presented in any format. It may be a movie, a book, a comic, a game or something else. Write down the essential concept of the story itself in 25 words or less.
- Evaluate the core story concept without any form of media or platform taken into consideration. This is all about the story. Is it RELEVANT and RELATABLE? Why and to whom? To move forward, you need to be able to answer these fundamental questions.

If the fundamental questions cannot be answered, there is the option to take a further step back, and take relevance, relatability and chosen audience into consideration. Then, revisit the core story description and change it if needed. Or, decide that this is not the right concept to bring to another platform.

With the chosen audience as a guiding light, decide on three different platforms to explore how the story may evolve. Platforms may be movies, interactive videos, games, comic books, virtual or real-life experiences, etc.

Note that the platforms need to be some that are used by the audience; before going deeper into design and development, you may need to do some research to find out what they actually use, rather than go for assumptions. It takes a monumentally powerful concept to make people shift their regular platforms; it can be done, but creators need to consider whether they want to add to the challenge of successfully launching the story experience.

> It takes a monumentally powerful concept to make people shift their regular platforms.

Work out how the story concept may work on each platform. An initial design can be roughs, a short description of the whole thing or of key moments. Present what the audience will experience, if possible, to a group of potential audience members.

Comparing the three new concepts, decide which one(s) deliver on each of the following demands:

- Does the concept on the new platform still represent the core story, perhaps in a new way?
- Does the concept on the new platform retain or preferably, enhance, relevance and relatability?
- Does the concept on the new platform come through as a believable experience, capable of creating a suspense of disbelief?

At the end of this experiment, there may be more than one concept that shows potential. The choice can then be made based on production capabilities or resources, or a combination of platforms may be explored to begin the design of a transmedia story experience across platforms.

CHAPTER 10

The Integrated Storytelling check list

Integrated Storytelling by Design is more than the sum of parts. It is a combination of balanced elements used to design and create rich and engaging story experiences by applying the best of multiple disciplines to create a coherent, harmonious whole.

In order to do this, and to venture beyond the telling of stories to story experiences that are not defined or limited by formats, media or technology, the following ten crucial criteria should be considered and implemented by designers and creators to various degrees, depending on the specifics of a story experience project.

Audience-Centric Design: The audience is always at the centre of the design process.

Story Experience: Integrated Storytelling has a strong, integrated story experience concept that balances the story with the experience.

Audience Influence: The story experience designers consider and often utilise audience influence to the story at various points before or during the story experience.

Audience Context: The design of story experience considers the audience context, such as location and modality; where they are and what they are doing.

Creator-Story-Audience Relationship: The story experience design challenges the traditional relationship between the creator, the story and the audience with an audience-centric design approach.

Story Modularisation: The story experience is constructed as a series of modules that can be combined and applied differently for various kinds of storytelling, such as digital, non-linear and interactive storytelling.

Interdisciplinary Design: The story experience is created with interdisciplinary skills and disciplines simultaneously and seamlessly, making for the creation of hybrid story experiences that combines different elements and settings, such as the digital and the physical world.

Transmedia Convergence: The story experience is interconnected across media, meaning that the same content is not merely replicated from one platform to the next; each adds to the richness of the combined story experience in its own way.

Technology Independent: The concept of the story experience is not based on a singular current technology but can apply new technologies or other future possibilities.

Organisationally Integrated: The story experience is created with the organisation that will bring it to life and operate it, often through close collaboration or co-creation sessions, so the operation and living of the story derives from or becomes a natural part of the organisational, or brand, DNA.

The above-mentioned ten key criteria can be balanced and combined differently depending upon how they help make the best, most relevant audience-centric story experience for a specific project. Those seeking a secret formula to Integrated Storytelling, given its many possible combinations and dynamics, will find that there is no one single solution.

The above is part of a design framework to elicit key questions for creators designing an Integrated Storytelling experience. This includes assessing how important each of these criteria is in the overall concept and whether they are achieved at the level intended or not. Not all of them need to be of high priority, but those that are needs to work, and work absolutely well.

Part II
Design

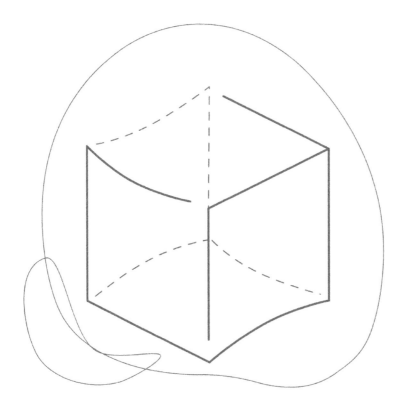

"*A true artist is not one who is inspired, but one who inspires others.*"

Salvador Dali

CHAPTER 11

The audience is the hero!

The Hero's Journey is a common narrative model used for a broad category of tales involving a hero who goes on a transformative adventure. Also referenced as a monomyth, it is widely applied as a foundation for the dynamics of a hero-centric story, in particular, for movies.

The study of the hero myth began in 1871 with anthropologist Edward Burnett Tylor's observations of patterns in plots of heroes' journeys and was made popular by Joseph Campbell,[1] who was influenced by Carl Jung's view of myth. In his 1949 work The Hero with a Thousand Faces, Campbell described the basic narrative pattern of a Hero's Journey as a series of steps that takes the hero from the ordinary to the extraordinary world and back, with an adventure that begins once the hero answers to the call of adventure. During the adventurous journey, fears and dangers must be overcome for the hero to return to the ordinary world and being rewarded by taking his or her rightful place in it.

The Hero's Journey is often depicted as a circular model, where the hero travels in a circle from the ordinary world to the extraordinary world and back again. The journey is not just the outer action such as fighting trolls, villains and other malevolent forces that need to be slain to restore order. It is also an inner journey that portrays the personal and character development of the protagonist that undertakes the journey. Furthermore, the structure of the Hero's Journey at its core already has a deeper connection with audiences, as it follows the same path as a personal crisis: an event disrupts a person's ordinary world, he or she chooses to face the challenge it presents, things often get worse before they get better, until finally he or she establishes a new ordinary world to inhabit it as a renewed, better person. As pointed out previously, audiences get drawn in by an emotional connection to the main characters, and even the most fantastic worlds and adventures hold comments to our ordinary lives and

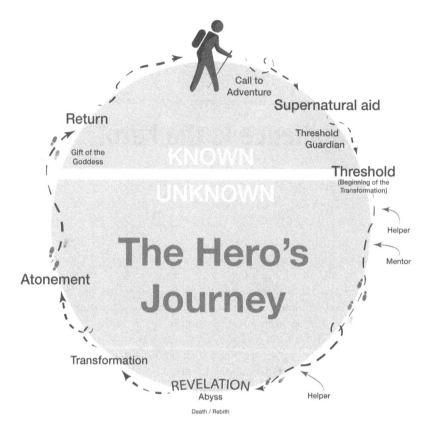

Call to
Adventure

Supernatural aid

Return

Threshold
Guardian

Gift of the
Goddess

KNOWN

Threshold
(Beginning of the
Transformation)

UNKNOWN

The Hero's
Journey

Helper

Mentor

Atonement

Transformation

REVELATION

Helper

Abyss

Death / Rebirth

The Hero's Journey.

world problems. In other words, the journey acts as an inner and outer journey for the protagonist as well as a mirror for the audience.

Even if one does not know the specifics of this model, it will be almost certainly recognisable, as it is often used to structuring a storyline, often to the point of formulaic use as is arguably the case with many Hollywood movies. As with any other model, the outcome from its application becomes more innovative and original when it is used as a dynamic tool, not as a rigid set of rules; it can be utilised for creating plot twists, misdirecting the audience into expectation of an event that would usually take place according to the Hero's Journey structure, just to surprise them by letting something else happen. As with any other method, mastering it means being able to alter it for one's own purpose, and learning more about this model, in particular, is highly recommendable, as it can be translated into a design model for sequential experience design. When doing so, audiences can literarily walk in the footsteps of the hero, immersed as a character in the story.

THE AUDIENCE JOURNEY

In his book *Every Guest Is A Hero*, Adam M. Berger[2] introduces The Hero's Journey as a method for creating an experiential, spatial journey through the Disney theme parks, altering the role and the passage of the audience as they are physically placed in the story universe. Just as is the case with customer journeys from commercial experience design,[3] an audience journey can be constructed as a sequence of steps of the audience making their way through the narrative and the context that it exists within.

> When the audience actually enters a themed physical or virtual space, they are literarily getting into the story, and for this, the models for narrative designs need to be developed further.

The state of emotional and mental immersion into a book, film, etc., is often referred to as 'getting into the story'. When the audience actually enters a themed physical or virtual space, they are literarily getting into the story, and for this, the models for narrative designs need to be developed further. Once inside the story, the audience will no longer settle for a passive role, standing on the sideline, merely watching. Ultimately, they become the lead protagonists, as their journey takes them from novice to celebrated hero, and they get to influence the story world they travel. They need to be allocated a vital role inside the Hero's Journey, as it is transformed into the Audience Journey, in which the audience is the hero.

One issue that then arises with the often-used circular Hero's Journey model is that it lacks ability to take the evolution of the audience into consideration because it is centred around the story and the hero within, not the audience. Regardless of whether the story is encountered for the first, second or third time, it still depicts the same journey from ordinary to extraordinary world and back. However, the journey itself influences the audience. Once they have travelled the narrative for the first time, there is no return to the same point of origin. You cannot do anything for the first time twice; consider the first time encounters with movies with overwhelming and

> The journey itself influences the audience. Once they have travelled the narrative for the first time, there is no return to the same point of origin. You cannot do anything for the first time twice.

surprising plot twists, such as the revelation of Keyser Söze's identity in *The Usual Suspects* or the identity of the murderer in Alfred Hitchcock's *Psycho*, the surprise thrill when going around a corner on a theme park ride, the first significant weapon found in Doom, Ratchet & Clank or other video games or the jump scares of a haunted house or horror flick.

The list goes on, and you may want to relive the moment, but it will be without the same element of surprise. You may want to revisit it with friends and family to relive the moment through them, but still, there's only one first time for everything.

This is where a dynamic story experience adds new value to the Audience Journey. Compared to a book or a film, interactive content in any format is capable of going beyond the repetition of doing everything the exact same way. The audience may be recognised as someone who has completed certain levels of understanding of how to interact in a specific setting and will be treated as such. Or, there may be many different pathways through the experience, meaning that one will not see and experience everything in the same way as the first time around. This may even extend to the level of having multiple storylines connected to an overall meta-story. The storylines themselves may be living, organic or updatable, so that when the audience descends into their extraordinary worlds, new storylines and experiences await even repeat visitors.

A single, circular motion from the ordinary to the extraordinary and back such as the Hero's Journey is an essential narrative tool. However, it can hardly contain all the dimensions and possibilities of current and future storytelling platforms, and that is why there is a need to develop a new framework for the story experience and the audience journey passing through it. It requires thinking of a story as a design structure to enable the audience to not only experience, but also influence the story experience as they travel through it along different pathways. One such immersive story structure is the Story Sphere.

NOTES

1. Joseph Campbell: The Hero with a Thousand Faces (1949)
2. Adam M. Berger: Every Guest Is A Hero (2013)
3. Customer journey: refers to the path followed by a customer via touchpoints before making a purchase.

CHAPTER 12

Constructing immersive narrative designs with Story Spheres

When taking the next step from mentally and emotionally connecting people to the story to actually placing them in it, one way often used is to surround the audience with an environment, themed with recognisable elements, scenes and characters, as seen in theme parks or virtual environments. However, surrounding the audience with the features of the story is not necessarily the same as immersing them within the narrative itself. Even in the middle of a 360-degree environment, the audience can be still be travelling as mere observers who do not really take part in the narrative itself – they are still distanced from it, not capable of influencing the events around them.

In established or traditional communications or narrative models used such as when a brand conveys a message to the customer, or a storyteller presents a story to an audience on a screen or a page, the audience is on the outside looking into an intriguing series of events.

However, when inviting the audience inside to become part of the story, the story universe and the audience universe converge into one space in which story and audience are mutually influential.

With the audience journey now placed inside this universe, their passage through all the layers of the story influences how it unfolds. For a better understanding of this relationship, the layers of the story can be defined as a Story Sphere that can visualise story structures for a long line of platforms and media. Here, the audience is invited into a living and breathing story universe containing a multitude of objects that can be interacted with and in doing so, spark the creation of a series of different storylines, multiplied by perspectives and pathways.

> The audience is invited into a living and breathing story universe.

STORY SPHERE LAYERS

The Story Sphere.

The layers of the Story Sphere make up the immersive story and its components, regardless of media and whether it is physical, virtual or a hybrid of the two. The layers are placed around a conceptual core acting like a gravitational pull keeping the structure together. Without a strong core, the layers tend to drift apart, and the story itself becomes hollow.

The Story Sphere is constructed by a series of main layers so that each of them can contain several sublayers. The main layers are, from the centre and outwards.

The core story concept or premise at the centre is the anchoring and origin of all other layers. As mentioned above, it needs to have enough gravitational pull to keep everything together and attract audiences.

The storyline consists of elements such as plots, subplots and genre-specific story devices. Often, a storyline consists of more than a singular story to add depth and perspective to the overall story experience.

The characters are relatable connection points to the audience, regardless of whether the characters are heroes, villains or others.

The creatures such as animals, beasts and beings without the same level of intelligence that the characters have. They can cross the border into characters, not only in animated features where animals take on human characteristics but also as animals that are key characters without being humanised the same way. One example is the loyal animal being a main character.

The objects can have a variety of functions from being part of the environment to changing the course of the storyline. They can include various props, stones, cars, spaceships and the pivotal gun that will ensure the advancement and success of the protagonist. Props can sometimes take on characteristics of creatures, even sentient beings, become an essential character or be so vast, that it becomes a space. Think of the horrors of houses and spaceships seemingly coming alive.

The space is the placeholder for scenes, different levels, etc. It can be as small as a room or as vast as a galaxy. Stories, games and experiences often take the audience from one space to the next in a sequence to underline the advancement of and differentiation within a story or a game. Multiple spaces can coexist in a Story Sphere.

The world is sometimes referred to as storyworld and can be achieved through elaborate worldbuilding. It sets a more tremendous scene for different spaces with depth is added with environments, social structures, inhabitants, etc. The term world can be used in both singular and plural, such as when constructing sci-fi or fantasy storyworlds that hold multiple worlds within. In some sci-fi scenarios, worlds are treated as spaces, with only one setting per planet.

The universe – sometimes referenced as the storyverse – is a broader concept than describing a particular universe that holds individual planets or galaxies defined by worldbuilding. The story universe is what defines the universal rules for a story experience and what is possible. From a design perspective, it is the definition of possibilities and constraints set by genres: magic is a possibility in a fantasy realm; space travel is a regular theme in science fiction and so on. New hybrid genres are created by combining existing genres such as steampunk that combines a Victorian-themed universe with that of the what-if premise of science fiction to present adventures in an alternative timeline.

It is easy to treat the above as a rigidly defined set of rules or a formula. One should consider, though, what interesting dynamics may happen when altering the elements to become anachronisms or changing the rules in other ways. The audience may realise that a house is haunted which can elevate it from scene to prop to creature to an essential antagonistic character. The universal rules may change to the surprise of the audience, such as when a road movie turns into a horror flick, Quentin Tarantino's *From Dusk To Dawn* being one example where an exotic dancer suddenly turning vampire marks the transition.

> Sometimes, hybrid concepts may define a new kind of universe.

Sometimes, hybrid concepts may define a new kind of universe, such as in the Korean television series Kingdom, which is part feudal historical drama, part zombie apocalypse in a manner that even combines the usual beautiful scenarios of the first genre with the grittiness of the latter. As audiences make their way through the Story Sphere, they may find both their perception of how a story can be experienced, and what its universe may contain, to be challenged.

CREATING STORY SPHERES IN COLLABORATION

It takes a team to make a Story Sphere come alive up until and after it is opened to the public. The foundation of the concept and the story needs to be elaborated and produced in full detail, media assets need to be produced, and engineering and programming needed to realise the vision in physical, virtual or hybrid spaces has to be developed, tested and implemented.

For each specialised expert, individual or in a group, the anchoring point for common understanding is based on a shared idea of what the audience experience is. This kind of audience-centric design narrative will be explored further in Part V of this book, and the consequential considerations for planning and managing an Integrated Storytelling project will be discussed, in further detail, in Part VI.

CHAPTER 13

From theory to practice: Constructing a basic Story Sphere

In order to construct a Story Sphere, the first steps are to define its inner core and its outer frame before populating it with the layers and subsequent elements that will become parts of a rich story experience. The core is the Core Story Concept, the basic idea that everything should gravitate towards. The outer frame is the Universe, the setting that defines universal rules for every layer inside it.

First and foremost, a strong core story concept needs to be in place. As a creator, you will have to ask yourself why this story needs to be told, what is the heart in it and why would it be relevant to your audience? Based on these considerations, a core concept should be written down in the most economical way. One very effective method is the make a High Concept description of 25 words or less. One example could be:

> *A prodigal son returns to his childhood home to find it overtaken by enemies that he must fight to learn the fate of his family.*

This basic premise and protagonist struggle contain several possible scenarios of character conflict, development and resolution. Once the Universe layer is added, specifics and uniqueness are added to the story experience, while keeping the focus on the character persistent. What would it mean to the story if the Universe were a small Wild West town? Is it an early-twenty-first century conflict in Europe or a fictional version of the United States, perhaps based on alternative history? What if the Universe is the literal universe travelled by our descendants thousands of years from now?

The Core Story Concept and the Universe layers create a framework inspiring the creation of more details, characters, objects, etc. Once we work with the other layers, they become influential, though, even to the

The Story Sphere.

point where you may choose to challenge the universe or slightly tweak the Core Story Concept.

As a design structure, elements can be defined and replaced before the story is presented as one or more storylines. One way of exploring this is through taking these steps, where one layer is changed to change key elements surrounding the same core concept:

- Define a Core Story Concept as described above.
- Define the Universe that establishes the rules for the story world in which the events will take place.
- Define and describe some key Characters, Creatures and Objects and how they will help the protagonist achieve his or her goals.
- Based in the above, write a short storyline.
- Change the Universe.

- Define and describe some key Characters, Creatures and Objects, and how they will help the protagonist achieve his or her goals, now based on the redefined Universe.
- Write a new short storyline.

What differences and similarities do you find?

The options can also be put into a table that allows you to compare how different Universes may unfold. The example below showcases the prodigal son concept in a science fiction, contemporary action and a Wild West genre scene. These are obviously optional and can be changed, even challenged even further. What if the Universe was a romantic comedy?

Fill out as many elements as possible before proceeding to the storyline, to explore how the Universe setting may differentiate and influence the storyline once populated with the elements in each layer.

	Universe A: Science fiction	Universe B: Contemporary action	Universe C: Wild west
Core story concept	A prodigal son returns to his childhood home to find it overtaken by enemies that he must fight to learn the fate of his family.		
Characters			
Creatures			
Objects			
Space			
World			
Storyline			

Stories as design structures enables the creator to design variations by exchanging elements, without having to write storylines from one end to the next. This process is essentially circular and non-linear creation. It is possible to move back and forth between layers and reimagine elements in the early concept development process, even to the point of shifting Universe, if the story fits one better than the other.

This process is essentially circular and non-linear creation.

Circling back and forth will reveal the best option through exploration before detailed scripting begin.

The importance of setting a timeframe for this kind of creative development has to be noted, though. Setting a deadline will help creators not getting stuck in a perpetual loop of exploring their concept.

Working with elements in the Story Sphere as described above, also paves the way for dynamic narratives, such as interactive and non-linear storytelling, where choices made by the audience set the direction for, or even create pathways through multiple storylines. It does so by adding the possibility of re-arranging story elements and giving them different attributes.

The story has now become a structure of Micro Stories in combination rather than a traditional narrative structure with events arranged in one way through beginning, middle and end.

CHAPTER 14

Creating new narrative structures and dynamics with Micro Stories

As is often the case with any progress, new narrative dimensions are reached standing on the shoulders of giants, often a part of an evolution rather than a revolutionary departure. From the early cave paintings and the shamanistic traditions of oral storytelling through the narrative models developed by the ancient Greeks to the mediation and subsequent digitalisation, the next steps in storytelling are exactly that; next steps that continue a route laid down aeons before. When we take them, we do not ignore what has already been defined, or the disciplines that have been thoroughly developed and applied across media types. The new generation of story creators should not be ignorant of well-established and well-working principles, because it provides the groundwork when engaging with new formats and possibilities. While storytelling by design provides the power to unlock new possibilities, having a well-established toolbox of traditional storytelling skills will add depth and relevance when exploring and presenting these new possibilities to an audience. You need to know the rules to expand on them, not to mention break them.

While keeping the fundamentals in mind, due to new technologies and their adoption by not only the creators, but also more significantly the audiences, now is a pivotal moment in the history of storytelling and story experiences. The current evolution goes beyond the mediation, presentation and the distribution of narratives to how interaction with their elements can change their very structure. Structures that may not even be defined as constants, but as interchangeable in ever-evolving patterns. Such narratives become organic; the new generation of living stories.

> The current evolution goes beyond the mediation, presentation and the distribution of narratives.

RESTRUCTURING STORYLINES AS COMBINATIONS OF EVENTS

Can a story be interactive or not? The answer is far from a simple yes or no.

Considering AI, how it can enhance a story cannot be uncovered in-depth by such a simple negative or positive statement; a deeper understanding, and, thus, explanation of how AI can be implemented at different levels is needed. In parallel and often symbiotic with interactive narratives, non-linear storytelling encompasses more nuances and options, all tied to interaction and choices made by the audience throughout the storylines they travel. The new storytelling formats are immensely nuanced and intertwined to become combinations of story experience possibilities; digital and interactive, digital and interactive and non-linear, etc.

To make detailed choices when working with the complexity of formats and possibilities they represent, it is necessary to deconstruct established narrative structures into smaller events.

For the story experience creator to make detailed choices when working with the complexity of formats and possibilities they represent, it is necessary to deconstruct established narrative structures into smaller events, each with their own attributes. They may then be rearranged individually or grouped in variations that create multiple string variations. This practice has its roots in experience design, where a granulated step-by-step view is often needed to review and if necessary, redesign an experience, as experiences do not only consist of one event, but several events happening in sequence, sometimes in parallel. If you were to describe a ride, a party, a performance, etc., you would be describing the part events that they are combinations of, like entry, seating, socialising, highlights, low points and exit.

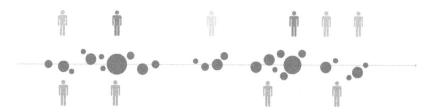

Event clustering can make experiences, stories and services confusing and hard to handle.

Each event that in combination make up the overall experience have different meanings, lengths and impacts. A combination of smaller events can represent just as much value as a larger event. Related to the definition integration discussed earlier in this book, they all converge into one harmonious – or disharmonious – whole, which can have a lasting positive or negative impact as a memory.

The Disney theme parks have worked with what they call Magic Moments for decades.[1] It was established as a way for the Disney employees to act on the observations they made on the frontline of working side-by-side of the visitors. Within a setting that presents the visitors with a multitude of different main events – including the closing show at night, which is a literal main event – Magic Moments are all the small positive things that can be done to better the visitor experience. It may be pointing out a better spot for a family to view the parade, or it may be the kindness to a tired child by someone who stays in character but acts on empathy rather than from a script. Some of the Magic Moments may be so seemingly insignificant that the visitors simply think of them as a natural part of being engaged in a well-hosted, well-serviced experience.

> In combination, all the small moments have the potential to build our perception of places and people.

However, in combination all the small moments have the potential to build our perception of places and people as being positive or negative without being easily recalled in every detail. The latter may be the reason why the Magic Moments are so impactful; they are seeded directly somewhere between the conscious and the subconscious.

There is research available that relates to the dynamic of the moment creator and those who experience the moments; whereas, the designer deconstructs or constructs and granulates and event into smaller moments to construct a harmonious whole, the audience does not necessarily see every little moment, but the bigger picture. In their book 'The Power of Moments', Chip Heath and Dan Heath explore and references research on this phenomenon.[2] If Disneyland visitors were asked in intervals throughout their stay how high they would rate their current state of satisfaction with an experience from a scale from one to ten, the averages may end up between 6 and 7, with a major event on a ride and buying mouse ears for the kids before leaving both being among the highest-rated moments. However, if asked after the visit how they would rate the experience, the rating may be higher than 9, due to the high level of influence of the two most memorable moments or defining moments for how the day is imprinted in our memory. One may ask why buying the mouse ears have such high influence. It is because of *when* it happens; at the end of the experience, wrapping up the day.

In parallel, for travel and hospitality, a defining moment is when the guest enters the hotel room for the first time. Possibly weary after travel, being positively reaffirmed or surprised defines the immediate expectations for the rest of the stay, and of course, the scale is tipped the other way around, when the hotel room is revealed for the first time. The overall impression is defined when it is time to leave again, such as the final evening at the hotel, and even though guests will look back on every part that has made up their experience, the successfulness of that final day in itself will have a significant influence on the overall perception. Key moments in the experience are not only situated at the beginning. The end is also of the outmost importance.

When designing an experience as a structure built from moments, insights like what is mentioned above adds to the understanding of what makes moments different. Negative or positive, they have different significance and impact, which as stated above is not only defined by *what* happens, but *when* it happens.

Relating experience design as described here to storytelling, a story may have many events of deep meaning and impact, but if there is no defining moment for getting into the story – a point of no return for the audience, they will never get to this content. Furthermore, not leaving them with a parting event of significance may influence how the story experience is remembered. It may not end with a satisfying high note, or the direct opposite; it ends too abruptly. Or, referencing The Hero's Journey, when there is no proper road back to The Ordinary World, the audience is just dumped back into it, often with frustration or confusion.

When there is no proper road back to The Ordinary World, the audience is just dumped back into it, often with frustration or confusion.

Integrated Storytelling begins with the story and the experience, and not necessarily one after the other. The granulation of the experience into moments mirrors the story if we look at story structures as a combination of events. Both are harmonious combinations of a series of moments and events that can be identified as unique elements that can have various significance and attributes. Furthermore, these elements can be rearranged in a multitude of ways in order to create a multitude of new storylines and experiences.

MICRO STORIES AND MODULAR STORYTELLING

The concept of stories being made up as a convergence of events or moments, adds modularity to a story that allows for looking at each element as a point of engagement and influence; not only towards the audience, but also from the audience and ultimately

The concept of stories being made up as a convergence of events or moments, adds modularity to a story that allows for looking at each element as a point of engagement and influence.

two-way interaction. Furthermore, this modularity also presents a way to unfold a story across various platforms and media in non-linear ways.

Stories can be deconstructed in multiple ways to become modular designs. Working within the Story Sphere as the setting, the story experience itself can be extended across platforms and locations. The narrative structure may be similar to the steps of the Hero's Journey, which can all be transferred from their circular structure into modules along a line. Each of these modules work individually and in combination, constructed with their own narrative structures with a beginning and an end, comparatively simpler than the overall storyline they may be part of. The modules have become Micro Stories, each with the possibilities for audience interaction and influences in unique ways. Think of game design, where on part may be storyline, one part may be exploration and one part may be a fighting or action sequence. Each of these steps has different levels and types of audience agency.

Each step of The Hero's Journey can be deconstructed into Micro Stories.

In a theme park setting, the Micros Stories are found throughout the park, often in dedicated zones, that are themed in a way that sets the style and genre for the Micro Story, keeping it relevant in that particular setting.

Regarding transmedia, the Micro Stories are encountered across multiple platforms, and the more the audience picks up, the richer their experienced storyworld becomes. The Micro Stories can be presented in various media and be compatible with various audience contexts and modalities. The definition of transmedia does not hold a demand for interaction, so the audience experience can be one of passive observation from books to movies to comics and so on and so forth. The important aspect is that the richness of storyworld built through each engagement point with the audience is not merely by replication of content but through adding further related perspectives, storylines, spin-offs, etc.

Modular Storytelling, in game design, holds a vast potential of a more profound merging of story and interaction. A typical game story structure is story (introduction and instruction) – game – story (cut scene) – game – story (cut scene) and so on until one or multiple variations of endings are reached. Even in less obvious game/story structures, the players are often presented with a similar structure, now combining a high level of interactive action such as fighting adversaries with a lower level of interactive actions with explorative decisions when choosing direction or missions to take.

It is possible to design new kinds of story experiences when elements of story and action co-exist with a simultaneous balance of either. In order to make this work, it will be necessary to change priorities not to make the experience a cognitive and interactive mess that will emerge the audience in confusion and overload rather than in an entertaining scenario. The story and the experience cannot be overly complicated when happening at the same time. The elements need to be near-perfectly balanced.

> The story and the experience cannot be overly complicated when happening at the same time.

Achieving the balance between the layers of the story experience is part of the process of designing it, but it is also a guiding light for the creator in choosing what should be interactive, how and to which extent.

BREAKING THE RULES TO BUILD DYNAMIC STORYLINES

As any storyteller, regardless of his or her media, will confess, a story is not just a story; it has its unique attributes, form and specific appeal. Genres aside, the infinite routes for the characters to travel and race the clock along storylines with various plots provide an opportunity and a possibility to challenge the norms and expectations and provide the audience with surprise and excitement. Sometimes, the universal rule in a Story Sphere for a specific genre is broken intentionally, ranging from the breaking of the fourth wall, where characters address the audience directly to the shift of genre within a story, which alters the universal rules unexpectedly. This goes beyond genres such as time travel tales, where, e.g. different time periods are naturally framed by the possibility of travelling from period to period as a universal rule in itself with the different time periods being the worlds that are visited.

The movie *From Dusk till Dawn* is a popular example of breaking or altering the universal rule of the genre that the story is seemingly set within from the beginning. The story begins as a road movie with two criminals on the run, who force a small family into helping them escape the law by going to Mexico. Once the small group makes it across the border to the rendezvous point, the rowdy Titty Twister bar, the story and genre change fundamentally as the day becomes night and the road movie surprisingly and instantly changes into a vampire horror story. Now the small group have to put their diversities aside and fight alongside other humans at the bar to survive until dawn. This shift creates a unique and surprising dynamic to the movie and is a proof that narrative bravery like that could be applied to even pop culture movies without disheartening the audience.

In other cases, the story creator teases that things may not be what they seem, and compared to the sudden shift occurring in *From Dusk till Dawn*, hints and anticipation are laid out across the storyline to make the audience ask if things are not what they seem. What if the crazy man postulates about an alien invasion is actually reality such as in – Warning! Spoiler alert – 10 Cloverfield Lane. Such mechanics apply very well to storylines that unveil reality to be horror or science fiction, or conspiracy to be reality. In order to break the universal rule and surprise the audience as in the case with *From Dusk till Dawn*, a noticeable if not seismic shift from one set of universal rules to the other has to happen at a specific point in the story experience. When well crafted, it can be a hit with audiences and critics alike, sometimes even creating a new kind of sub-genre or even a genre in its own right. Imagine the amplification of this impact to the audience, when they are actually inside the story, realising that it is revealed that it is something else than expected.

Set in the dynamics of Integrated Storytelling, rule-bending can add even more to the story experience. It is essential to keep in mind that too much of it – just as in the case of movies, etc., – can create confusion and lower the desire for engagement from the audience.

This may happen when fresh and innovative ideas give in to downright silliness and overcomplication, making the concept unrelatable and devoid of attracting a significant positive interest. When the empathy with people fails, the Integrated Storytelling project becomes a narrative experiment for a limited group, and not a story design to be experienced by a wider audience.

When the empathy with people fails, the Integrated Storytelling project becomes a narrative experiment for a limited group, and not a story design to be experienced by a wider audience.

Adding the value needed, storylines, worlds and universal rules can be influenced by the audience to the point of changing the story experience considerably. Thinking of story elements from storylines to characters as modules and possible points of interaction sets a direction for how interaction can go further than that of a bonus counter as known from video game designs. Part of the relatability and attraction is the possibility for the audience to shape their story experience.

WORLD AND UNIVERSE INFLUENCE AND INTERACTION

Taking the audience agency to other levels, influencing and interacting with the worlds and the universe makes even more unique and personalised story experiences possible. Especially in game design, the world that is explored can be one of designed by the player, using a toolbox provided by the game designer, rather than a space defined by the game designer. Even what the spaces are used for may be controlled by the player, with Minecraft being an example of influence to the point of co-creation is evolving at the discretion and empowerment of players.

Choosing various strategies for the width and depth of audience interaction is not just something that applies to gaming. Experience design has evolved beyond the gaming and the attractions industry. It is not limited to user and service design either, but can help create deeper engagement in marketing, training, learning, etc.

- A social worker might be trained in dangerous situations by being immersed in a storyline that suddenly changes from a scenario of guidance of a citizen in need to counter-action of the threat posed by a citizen being erratic and violent.
- Experiencing the message in Experiential Marketing may be enhanced by the enhanced reality world around potential customers changing due to them aligning with the activating brand.

And, learning may become a gamified experience on a mainstream scale, providing students with an immersive and interactive learning environment.

Going beyond an arguably widespread understanding that new ways of experiencing storytelling are limited to entertainment opens up a world of possibilities to other industries and may even create some new ones. Storytelling is indeed becoming more than what it was.

NOTES

1. Lee Cockerell: Creating Magic (2008)
2. Dan Heath & Chip Heath: The Power of Moments: Why Certain Experiences Have Extraordinary Impact (2017)

CHAPTER 15

From theory to practice: Structuring Micro Stories

By breaking down a storyline to a series of moments that can work on their own and in various combinations, a story experience can be experienced by the audience in a multitude of ways.

These moments, which were introduced on the preceding pages as Micro Stories, can be made up as entirely new modules, or be based on an existing narrative that is deconstructed into modules to come to life in a new way. Furthermore, each module may be experienced in different ways by the audience that may be assigned different functions and modalities associated with each little piece of the story. When building a constellation of Micro Stories, it is imperative to design them as pieces of a puzzle that can fit together in different ways, as they may be encountered differently and in a different order.

The key elements of the Micro Stories are content, context and control: what part of the overall story does it contain, what context or order is it encountered in, and what kind of control and influence the audience has in interacting with it.

Each module has an entry and an exit point that help build connection between the Micro Stories. At the entry point, what the audience know or feel, or in other words, their rational and emotional state, is highly influential of their story experience. Consider the case of a murder mystery. The audience may have left an exit point where they have picked up an essential clue, and are now one step closer to solving the case, which has lifted their sense of intrigue and determination to solve the case. They are kept engaged with the story experience.

Micro Stories, in context with others, also have various levels of importance in moving a story forward. Some of them may contain elements that are mandatory for understanding or moving the story forward, hence the consideration of what the audience will bring with them from one exit point to an entry point. Other Micro Stories may act to adding to the environment or providing subplots or further character exploration. They enrichen the storyworld, but the plot and the experience can move forward without them.

MODULISING THE MURDER OF MR. MCMONEY

As a working example, the classic murder mystery can be explored as a set of Micro Stories:

(1) Setting the scene for the victim, self-made billionaire Mr. McMoney.
(2) Presentation of Mr. McMoney's background as a ruthless moneymaker.
(3) Introduction of the conflict between Mr. McMoney and his ex-wife.
(4) The backstory of the conflict between Mr. McMoney and his ex-wife.
(5) Introduction of the conflict between Mr. McMoney and his former business partner.
(6) The backstory of the conflict between Mr. McMoney and his former business partner.
(7) Introduction of the conflict between Mr. McMoney and his estranged son.
(8) The backstory of the conflict between Mr. McMoney and his estranged son.
(9) The killing of Mr. McMoney.
(10) The discovery of Mr. McMoney's dead body.
(11) The introduction of the leading investigator, Detective Casey.
(12) Presentation of Detective Casey's background story.
(13) The investigation of the crime scene by Detective Casey.
(14) The first meeting between Detective Casey and Mr. McMoney's butler.
(15) The first meeting between Detective Casey and Mr. McMoney's ex-wife.
(16) The first meeting between Detective Casey and Mr. McMoney's former business partner.
(17) The first meeting between Detective Casey and Mr. McMoney's estranged son.
(18) The first clue uncovered by Detective Casey, leading to the first theory to solve the case.
(19) Whomever the first clue points to be found murdered.
(20) The discovery that leads to Detective Casey's second theory.
(21) Detective Casey summons the butler and the remaining suspects for a confrontation.
(22) During the confrontation, Detective Casey presents his discovery.

(23) The discovery leads to a suspect being revealed as the perpetrator.
(24) The perpetrator tries to escape.
(25) The perpetrator is stopped by police officers.
(26) Detective Casey has a final comment about why the perpetrator ended up being a murderer and how it could happen to many others.
(27) The murder of Mr. McMoney is solved.

This outline is a straightforward, chronological telling of the story with possibilities for a few flashbacks at points 4, 6, 8 and 12.

Re-arranging the order of the Micro Stories that the murder mystery may alter the audience experience significantly:

What if... the killer is Mr. McMoney's ex-wife, but her backstory with a violent and abusive husband is told before he is murdered? The audience may root for her not getting caught.
What if... the conflict between Mr. McMoney's estranged son is not revealed before the time of the solving of the case? The audience may then be taken completely by surprise by the horrific acts of a seemingly grieving son. Especially if they are presented with a red herring,[1] making them consider another suspect guilty, as the case is unravelled.
What if... the perpetrator is not caught by the police officers when trying to escape. This outcome may disappoint the audience, but can also act as a catalyst for the story living on in their minds – and in a possible sequel.

When reconstructing and arranging a murder story such as this as a modular story, each of the Micro Stories has to work on their own, while having a connection to another. They are not necessarily in direct continuation in a script, as something else from the storyverse may be encountered in-between. One person may experience one set of combinations, while another person may experience another, making either story experience individualised with some shared mandatory events.

As mentioned earlier, each Micro Story has an entry and an exit point that connects to what has happened before, and what will happen after it. As an alternative to creating a vast amount of script variations, or programme it into an interactive narrative for each and every Micro Story, they can be combined in groups. Each group is dedicated to a series of connected Micro Stories so that they can share entry and exit points as a group. The grouping for the murder of Mr. McMoney may be:

- Group One: Introduction of scene and characters.
- Group Two: The murder of Mr. McMoney.
- Group Three: Detective Casey's investigation.
- Group Four: The solving of the case.

Group One introduces the stage and the characters as a universal entry point. Group Two builds on that; the person who is being murdered is the self-made billionaire Mr. McMoney. Because of this murder, there is a reason for the investigation in Group Three, which will eventually lead to the solving of the case in Group Four.

By grouping the Micro Stories in groups with shared rational and emotional entry and exit points, it is possible the prioritise the Micro Stories. Which ones in one group should the audience experience before going to the next group, and which ones are not that important to avoid confusion. Creators of these kinds of grouped Micro Stories will often find that while there may be 12 Micro Stories, only eight of them are needed for the audience to obtain the necessary insight and emotion to continue to the next group.

That is the beauty and the challenge of Modular Storytelling; the story designer can arrange the modules in many different ways and provide multiple pathways through a variety of storylines.

It has to be stated clearly that the above is by far not the one and only solution for the modularisation of the murder mystery. That is the beauty and the challenge of Modular Storytelling; the story designer can arrange the modules in many different ways, and provide multiple pathways through a variety of storylines. The audience may be provided with alternative routes, and be able to influence the storyline, taking each group of Micro Stories in different directions to different outcomes.

Furthermore, a modular story structure may not be static because of the possibility of adding, removing or changing Micro Stories in a group, especially with digitally delivered content. This can add to the more popular parts of the story experience, and make up for the weaker ones, based on what can be observed from the engagement and interactions between the audience and the story.

RE-ARRANGE THE MURDER OF MR. MCMONEY

Now is a good time to prepare the Post-its® or a flowchart maker like the free online programme Diagrams.net. Arrange the steps of the murder mystery in a new way by grouping the Micro Stories differently to create a storyline that progresses in another way. The universal entry point may be during or after the murder, and the storyline may begin with a more elaborate introduction of characters in a part of the story preceding the time of the killing. When having decided the groups and their order, use it to prioritise the Micro Stories that need to be encountered, and which are less critical. Re-arrange again to build another modular story structure to compare the difference to the experience between the two, as experienced by the audience. What happens to The Murder of Mr. McMoney, once the structure is modulated in different ways?

NOTE

1. A red herring is a literary device that leads readers or audiences towards a false conclusion.

Part III
Audience

"No man ever steps in the same river twice, for it's not the same river and he's not the same man."

Heraclitus

CHAPTER 16

Audience layer compositions

The people intended to be reached and engage with, regardless of whether the vehicle is a story, message, or any content in general, may be defined by their context as customers, visitors, viewers, users or players. In the context of Integrated Storytelling, the unifying definition is the audience, regardless of which of the above definitions they are most related to, and the perception of the audience and their role is essential to create a successful story experience.

One may consider attributes like geography, demographics or psychographics as what defines one's audience. Many are used to utilising techniques segmentation or arch types to help gain a deeper understanding of who they are. To the story experience designer, understanding who the ideal audience is, and being able to define them and their relation on various levels to a particular narrative are not just useful. It is a necessary part of the design process.

However, even with a clear idea of who the audience is, and their likes and dislikes, as valuable as it is, when designing new ways of experiencing stories, it is just the beginning. Just as characters in a successful story, an audience needs to be defined as more nuanced and have more dimensions to them. Otherwise, they will stick out like a cardboard cut-out in a group of real, three-dimensional people; flat and one-dimensional, which will most likely lessen the empathic connection that could otherwise be established.

AUDIENCE LAYERS

Regardless of media, the standard in mediated storytelling is to let the audience gaze into the story and create an emotional connection with the characters, storylines and the storyworld within. With Integrated Storytelling, we want to invite them into the story, explore it and play a role in it.

The audience themselves have nuances that are what makes them real people with real lives, hopes and dreams. People are more than target audiences with an averaged set of attributes who are waiting to absorb the creations and fulfil the intentions of storytellers. Besides their traditional target group definitions such as demographics and psychographics, when creating storytelling by design, we need to consider their other layers of identity and personality.

> People are more than target audiences with an averaged set of attributes who are waiting to absorb the creations and fulfil the intentions of storytellers.

Although these layers are unique to every member of the audience, groups can be established from interests and layer similarities. In doing so, it is possible to work around the herculean, arguably impossible, task of customizing everything for each and every person in the audience individually, while avoiding trying to force the notion that everybody is somewhat the same. It is a departure that is necessary to create individual experiences. In the end, all experiences become personal memories, even the ones that are established in a social context. The scenario of possibilities can ultimately create an infinite list of detail even within a group of similarities, which will need either prioritisation, new ways of handling by AI or a combination of both.

Similar to the Story Sphere layers, the audience layers are built from the core and outwards with a range of main layers that each has its own set of sublayers. Given all the nuances of people, the audience sphere of

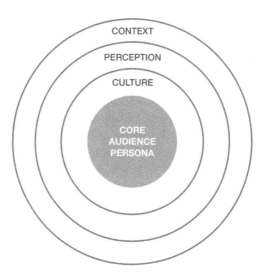

Sphere of audience layers.

layers appears deceivingly simple, as many of the layers are hidden as such sublayers within the primary layers. It is a model to build and elaborate from when used for specific audiences.

The core audience persona or personality is the unique combination of experiences, personal values, beliefs, hopes, dreams, likes and dislikes that makes up a person. When people see part of their personality reflected in a character or find a connection to a story or a space, a more profound connection is made between the audience and the story.

The audience culture is a set of shared codes and values that connects a group of people. Culture is not necessarily defined by proximity, nationality or race, although they can be highly influential. People can have more in common with someone on the other side of the world than their next-door neighbour. It is a testament to the power of the story how pop culture franchises like Harry Potter and Star Wars connect people from all around the world, whom all abide by the values, conduct and rituals of their fan culture. Culture also reflects our code of how we conduct ourselves as an audience, including but far from limited to our behaviour online or in the cinema. Some of the aggravations of going to the cinema are often caused by conflicting cultures; how people behave and expect others to behave may simply be different.

The audience perception is how the story is perceived and memorised by the audience influenced by to their own personality and culture. Perception can be granulated into several filters that are deeply coded within everyone and is highly influenced by the context of the audience; when and how we engage with the story. Keep in mind that the most potent story experiences can change or build a culture and even become transformational experiences, changing the perceptions, beliefs and values of even the core personality of the audience.

The audience context includes both what people do, and where they are; in other words, the audience modality and space. The context can be highly influential to the depth of immersion in the story; there is a big difference between sitting in the dark in a cinema, putting on a VR (Virtual Reality) Heads Up Display (HUD) or watching something on a smartphone while going from A to B on public transport.

Just like the Story Sphere layers, the audience layers could be applied in a formulaic manner or as a rigid structure. This would be limiting their potential, as the layers are more dynamic and mutually influential. A change in one layer can change another, even in real time as the story experience unfolds. Some creators use this to set a strategy of not just matching the core personality and culture, but to change it, such as immersive experiences designed as a call to action for environmental issues. Others play directly off the context of the audience, such as when designing location-based experiences that demand a certain kind of modality, platform and spatial awareness. The layers are part of an overall context of mutually influential factors that can enhance and amplify the impact and memorability of the story and the message it conveys.

CHAPTER 17

From theory to practice: Creating an audience code set

Recognising the audience codes that work for and against the intended story experience is a way to ensure compatibility, with connections and gaps working for or against it. As an example, wanting to transform the perception of the audience, an overview of what to improve and what to leave out creates focus and priority, rather than trying to take too many steps forward at the same time, which may leave your audience overwhelmed and discouraged.

To establish an audience code set, define and describe what you find in each of the audience layers:

The core audience persona: Describe the audience as an individual or a group of people. What are their values, interests, likes and dislikes? Is where they are in their life cycle in terms of work, education, family, etc., important to how they will connect to your story experience? Make a list of things that will work for you and a list of things that will work against you.

The audience culture: What cultural relations signify the audience? Are they highly influenced by where they are from? Is having a particular interest or franchise their strongest connection with others? Does their cultural relation mean they are for or against particulars that your story experience will represent? Add to the lists of things that will work for or against you.

The audience perception: What is the perception – or preconceived perception that the story will be met with by the audience? Will their opinion about the story matter, characters or, indeed, the creator influence their story experience even before it begins? Does this attract or push them away? Is the purpose to add or change their perception, and is this a feasible goal? Add to the lists of things that will work for or against you.

The audience context: When and where does the audience engage with the story experience, and how does that direct the way it is presented? Is time and space available for a deeper engagement in a dedicated place or tugging in at home? Is the story an additional element to a daily commute to and from work? Understanding the levels and limits of engagement at various audience touch points helps balance what is presented where, when and in what format. Complete the lists of things that will work for or against you.

Assess the lists of things that will work for or against you. If the balance is for, it could be a signal to proceed. If the balance works against you, you may need to consider how you can tip the balance or define a new audience. The result may show that only one of the layers are not promising, in which case you may want to try to change it to challenge the layer composition.

A combination of lists can prove useful for development and comparison. It can be one list of what audience codes are, and one of what you want them to be. It can be the codes for two various audiences to make their overlapping codes clear. The latter can be used for transforming a concept from one culture to another through cultural bridging, or when the purpose is to make different audiences come together. The basics of diplomacy arguable begin with discovering what similarities and common grounds can be found. This can also be applied when connecting audiences together.

CHAPTER 18

Designing connections across audience gaps

Even the best story structure may fail due to a gap between the creator and the audience. The first does not manage to attract or retain the attention of the other who in turn does not choose to invest time, money or both.

The audience layers can be viewed as filters that have to be bridged to create a connection with the audience. Challenging the connection may be the audience perception of the creator and the creator's offering, either of which may be deemed irrelevant for multiple reasons. The scepticism of why something is relevant to someone creates a notable gap between the creator, the audience and the story. With Integrated Storytelling, crossing the threshold and becoming part of the narrative is imperative and obviously demanding a motivated audience. This will not happen without connection and interest being established at an early point of awareness of the story experience being offered.

> With Integrated Storytelling, crossing the threshold and becoming part of the narrative is imperative and obviously demanding a motivated audience.

The distance set by the gap of indifference or perceived irrelevance between the creator and the audience can be widened even further to the point of the audience having an adverse and negative perception of the creator. The latter phenomena are no longer just a gap to be bridged through creating better awareness and understanding, but a wider chasm to be crossed, in which negative perceptions and even opposing views need to be changed. Sometimes, trying to bridge or cross either is abandoned because the effort outweighs the intended goal defined by purpose and strategy.

Early concept abandonment takes many forms. It includes theme park feasibility studies, where the investment in new attractions are calculated not to be able to make a profit or even make a deficit. Also included are the ever-present calculations in the movie industry, where the production and marketing costs have to be surpassed by ticket sales. In newer marketing disciplines, an initial infatuation of social media has given way to a more calculated and ROI-driven[1] investment in budget and resources with measurable KPIs[2] used to evaluate and drive the efforts of the marketing departments. All of these are outcomes of assessing success or failure. Despite what one may think, not moving forward can be positive, as money and resources that would most likely have been wasted can be put to good use elsewhere.

For the Integrated Storyteller, the possible gaps and chasms that have to be taken into consideration are a reminder that a great story – or story experience – does not come alive unless it is welcomed by and engaged with by an audience.

> A great story – or story experience – does not come alive unless it is welcomed by and engaged with by an audience.

There may be many reasons why that may not happen. Granted, there are plenty of stories of how the studio or the publisher was wrong in their assessment:

- J.K. Rowling had her first Harry Potter manuscript rejected 12 times, which after its publication paved the way for one of the most influential entertainment franchises of all time, with books, movies and theme parks as part of its universe.
- Warner Brothers shut down the production of Home Alone because of budget concerns, but the production of one of the most successful comedies of all time was immediately picked up by Fox, and the movie went on to make US$477 million at the box office against a production budget of US$18 million (IMDB) and got nominated for two Academy Awards (Oscars).
- Because of their previous work with George Lucas, Universal had an option of the original Star Wars movie, but they passed on it, eventually leaving the whole franchise with Fox.
- Beatles manager Brian Epstein's efforts to secure a contract for the band fell short with record labels including Columbia and HMV, and Decca Records famously rejected the band after an audition, which was recorded and eventually led to a record deal with EMI subsidiary Parlophone.

However, for each of these stories of bad decisions, there are plenty of stories about investments not being made where the common understanding is that the concept would have failed. For any professional creator, applying design thinking to a certain extent also means being willing to test, evaluate and leave behind that which does not work, at which point it is indeed time to Kill Your Darling.[3] The first step is not to understand whether the story will work according to narrative principles, or whether the experience will work according to experience design principles. The first step is to evaluate whether a connection can be made with the audience in the first place, motivating them to engage with the story and the experience.

CLOSING THE GAPS WITH THE GAP CONNECTION MODEL

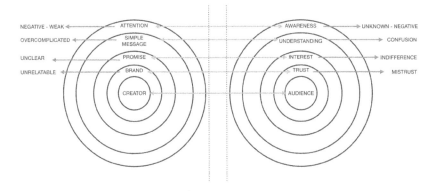

Gap Connection Model.

The above-mentioned Gap Connection Model is derived from a combination of the AIDA principle (Attention Interest Desire Action) and the Seven Elements of the Client's Decision Journey (Aware Understand Interest Respect Trust Able Ready).[4] It was designed to define possible connection points between the creator and the audience to bridge the gap that exists in the perception of the latter, to achieve positive open-mindedness towards the story, the message and the experience. The principle is to make the two gravitate towards each other, almost as two ships that are using ropes at various connection points to end up connected, alongside one another.

The opposite effect that is addressed with this model is that of the audience and the creator gravitating away from each other. The gap becomes a chasm, making the connection challenging if not an impossible exercise. As was the case in the previous From Theory to Practice exercise where the things working against making the connection might be overwhelming. If the gap is too wide, abandoning the concept may be advisable.

What is seemingly a marketing model can also be used as a way to establish a shared narrative and, therefore, the connection with the audience in a series of steps:

- The creator makes an effort to get the ATTENTION of the audience, who now have an AWARENESS of the creator. In contrast, invisibility due to the weak presence and negative attention can make this first step very steep to climb.
- The creator presents a SIMPLE MESSAGE that helps the audience's UNDERSTANDING of what it is the creator does. A typical communication error is that of overcomplicating things.
- The creator makes a PROMISE of how the wants and needs of the audience can be met by the creator, sparking and INTEREST from the audience, paving the way for taking affirmative action.
- The creator has a strong brand that makes the audience respect the creator's capabilities, good intention and TRUST in the creator to be the right choice to fulfil the PROMISE made earlier.
- At this point, the trust brand connection between the CREATOR and the AUDIENCE has been established, and action can be taken such as the audience investing time and money in engaging with and experiencing a story experience, making a purchase, support a cause, making a vote, etc.

For the model to achieve its full potential within the Integrated Storytelling framework, these steps are also to be perceived as steps in building a relationship between the creator and the audience. It is essential to keep in mind that the model is applied in an audience-centric concept, in which the communication and messaging to the audience from the creator has to be balanced with ample levels of interaction, with the creator operating in anticipation of and empathy of the wants, needs and actions by the audience. Hidden agendas and overt intentions − or in layman's terms, building a relationship on hidden truths or lies − can backfire spectacularly. In marketing, the brand promise is one of the most potent connection points with customers once accepted and anticipated. Breaking the brand promise is one of the most irreparable damages that can be made. In parallel, when people give you their time and money, you have to be prepared to deliver on your promise if the trust is not to be broken in the story experiences you create − and ultimately, yourself. That is

Breaking the brand promise is one of the most irreparable damages that can be made.

why it is so important to understand where and with whom you are more likely to live up to and exceed the expectations, and when it will take considerable extra effort.

NOTES

1. ROI: Return On Investment
2. KPI: Key Performance Indicators
3. Kill Your Darling refers to abandoning a favourite idea or concept.
4. Tom McMakin & Doug Fletcher: How Clients Buy (2018)

CHAPTER 19

Designing a creator – audience connection script

The Gap Connection Model can also be applied as part of a customer journey, depicting step-by-step interaction between the creator or brand and the audience, regardless of what the relationship between the two is. Mapping customer journeys is a popular and effective way of visualising and creating such steps and can be used to explore multiple possible outcomes. If we visualise the above journey as a journey map with various outcomes, it would appear something like a flowchart with multiple options throughout.

When storytelling is integrated as part of a relation-building effort between the characters involved (the creator and the audience). It adds further dynamic and emotional perspective, which is also useful to avoid formulaic sales mechanics similar to that of CRM[1] systems, in which the audience is often treated more like data than people. To add further perspective using Integrated Storytelling, the customer journey is enhanced by a script, describing a straightforward connection story with multiple outcomes. Based on the Gap Connection Model, the script used an example that of a story creator pitching an idea to a studio. To add human faces to the story, in the example below, the creator will be named Peter and the studio executive will be named Kathryn.

Attention

Kathryn has never heard of Peter, but Peter knows of Kathryn and her studio's need for taking a position in the popular fantasy genre in the wake of the success of Game of Thrones. Peter knows that getting through to Kathryn, who has a busy schedule, will be hard, so he decides against endless calls to secretaries and other gatekeepers.

Simple message

Instead, he chooses to let Kathryn experience what it is that he offers. Showing it rather than telling it. He puts together a physical mystery box that when opened, will unveil the new fantasy concept he has created. Knowing that everybody is looking for – and promoting their fantasy shows – as the next Game of Thrones, he decides to have a unique message. On top of the box it reads, with sparkling gold against the shiny black box material:

> It is time to move beyond Game of Thrones, and take the next steps forward in the magical evolution of fantasy storytelling.

The wordplay is bold, playing on the fact that an otherwise dedicated fan base was not all satisfied with the final season of the show. It is also stating that it is time to move on and create new unique shows that can challenge and move the fantasy genre forward, rather than launching Game of Thrones replacement shows.

When Kathryn receives the package, she does not open it right away but lets it sit at a desk in her office. In the package is hidden a simple device that plays sound at selected hours, starting with the bells of a huge clock, and then a short musical number referencing what the soundtrack may sound like. It is another bold move making sure that it the box is not forgotten, but also keeping with the theme of time to move beyond Game of Thrones and the proposed new fantasy franchise presented in further detail in the mystery box.

Promise

Curious by the sounds and music coming from the box, Kathryn opens it. Inside she finds an iPad that has a video presentation with a personal introduction by Peter. The concept he proposes is simple and powerful, one of those ideas that will have many wondering afterwards why they did not think of it. He makes part of his video presentation by him offering Kathryn the new iPad with the presentation as a present. It's an homage to an age-old way of establishing relationships, but also a traditional action by the mentors and mages of fairy tales, as they give the hero the secret potion, weapon or courage to assist in a quest to be accepted.

Brand

Among other things on the iPad and in the mystery box is a show reel of Peter's past productions, initial market research and other material, which supports the concept in being well developed and well researched even at this early point. The connection with the audience is ready to be established, hopefully lasting for a significant number of years.

Even with this innovative and impressive concept pitch, Peter does not wait around for Kathryn to get back to confirm a meeting. However, just as he is about to call her, she calls him. 'You have my interest', she says, 'let us meet and see what we can do with this'.

Connection

A week later, Peter comes by Kathryn's office for a meeting, which adds even further to the positive outcome for the new fantasy show, as Kathryn does not only buy into the concept but also Peter as a person. The agreement draft is in the mail.

In creating scenarios like these through the application of step-by-step scenarios, creative ideas and concept development presents themselves when writing the script. As does possible gaps and challenges, making it possible to address them proactively. In support of the concept and the story that is intended to be realised, a supporting narrative develops to help that realisation come through.

The example script above is written in the third person, but writing it from the perspective of Kathryn can add even more to the empathy with her and her point of view. When doing so, it is necessary to avoid being too speculative or too positively biased, such as exaggerating her interest towards excitement, as it may skewer the storyline in an unrealistic, rather than intended, direction. A change of perspective is to gain better understanding and empathy, including notions for and against that which is being presented.

NOTE

1. CRM: Customer Relationship Management

CHAPTER 20

The audience and the Integrated Story Sphere

CONNECTING THE STORY LAYERS WITH THE AUDIENCE LAYERS

To create a connection between the audience and the story, an interface is needed. By considering a multitude of ways of letting the audience engage with the story experience as interfaces, we maintain that Integrated Storytelling concepts are not just meant as a one-way presentation of the creator's vision, but provide a two-way connection point with the audience. A connection that may or may not contain interactivity and digital media, keeping in mind that interaction does not have to be digital. Theme park and improved theatre cast members are examples of personified human interaction.

The platforms chosen to interface the audience with the story experience are the specific connection points between the audience and the Story Sphere, and have a particular form such as a movie, game, theme park and so on. The constraints of a platform may have significant influence over the story experience and cause a need for alteration of multiple layers to make certain that the story fits the platform to provide the right experience. This way, the story and the story experience can be distributed across multiple platforms. However, it is essential to keep in mind that if the intent is to create connected, multi-platform transmedia, the role of every platform in combination needs to be considered. It is not adequate to simply replicate content from one platform to the next, not using each platform to their full potential in the process. A platform that does not play well with others may need to be disregarded.

> If the intent is to create multi-platform transmedia, the role of every platform in combination needs to be considered.

The level of audience influence is part of the considerations of the interface between the Story Sphere and the audience and is profoundly affected by which kind of interaction is provided by when interfacing with the audience. It may be a game or an interactive story, with features that influence the story experience. The evolution in the combination of the two may provide the grounds for a revolution in the creating of stories: one, in which the future of the creator lies not in storytelling, but in being able to design a framework for story experiences. In other words, the upcoming evolution of the story may not be driven by storytelling. Which leads to more advanced uses of models such as the Integrated Storytelling Story Sphere.

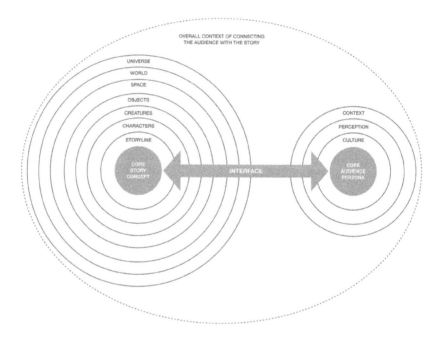

Connecting the Story Sphere with the sphere of audience layers.

DESIGNING THE INTEGRATED STORY SPHERE

To define an integrated model for designing story experiences that are created with the audience at the centre of their construction, the Story Sphere and the audience sphere can be merged into a new model which not only presents or surrounds the audience with the story, but is also influenced by them being at the core or the heart of it. This Integrated Story Sphere realigns the layers from the Story and Audience spheres and even contains a new kind of core structure. It contains an inner and an outer core. The inner and the outer cores represent the symbiotic duality of the audience and the story experience concept as each influence one another from the initial design to implementation and beyond. Working according to a design thinking mindset, achieving perfect balance is achieved through experimentation and circular development; as a result, despite what is widely recognised as an indisputable claim, the magic does not necessarily begin with the story. It may begin with the experience or the combination of both, as they will be lived by the audience. When creating non-linear, multi-disciplinary story experiences where the audience are positioned as the hero, to have an audience-centric, non-linear and multi-disciplinary design process with the audience at its centre is not just logic. It is a highly effective approach to explore and discover what combinations will work best.

Despite what is widely recognised as an indisputable claim, the magic does not necessarily begin with the story.

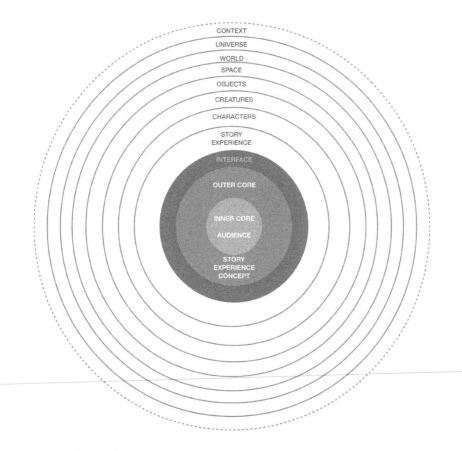

Integrated Story Sphere.

THE INTEGRATED STORY SPHERE FROM INNER CORE TO OUTER CONTEXT

At the inner core, the **audience** is the centre point with their personality, culture and other shared or individual layers.

At the outer core, the **story experience** concept completes the core of the Integrated Story Sphere. It is a double layer that balances the combination of experience and story. The story and the experience are highly mutually influential, and when working with story-based experienced, a back and forth development process balancing the two often needs to be utilised. The core story and the core experience are created in unison.

The **interface** between the core and story experience surrounds both the inner and the outer cores and consists of ways of interacting with the story. If the platform or the audience-story interaction design is not understandable, everything ends right here.

This layer and its sublayers may sometimes be more or less invisible to the audience. However, even without understanding the specifics of a failed interface, the audience understands when things do not work for them, and turn their backs to the story experience, whether it's a game, a ride in a theme park or something else. The interface layer can act as a bridge or enabler of the story experience, but also as a gap or deal-breaker. When it does not work, the confusion that can come from not being properly introduced to what the story experience is and how to engage with it, may discourage anyone form further engagement.

The interface is connected to the **story experience**, and how the story is experienced across multiple platforms and other story engagement points across time and space. The story experience consists of a combination of several narrative layers, most importantly the storyline narrative (the story in sequence) and the experiential narrative (the experience in sequence).

The consecutive layers are identical to the formerly introduced Story Sphere layers of **Characters**, **Creatures**, **Objects**, **Space**, **World** and **Universe** with one significant difference: what can be influenced by the audience at the core of the Integrated Storytelling Sphere and to what extent, has to be defined. The roles of the audience and their level of influence related to each of these layers is deeply rooted within the concept.

The story universe not only contains the story and experience elements. It reaches outwards, to the **context** in which the audience experiences the story. This has to be taken into consideration, as the context in terms of location and action is often more than a surrounding factor;

it is part of the experience, most notably when the audience can immerse themselves in virtual and physical worlds.

It should be repeated that rather than using this or any model in this book as a formula, it should be considered a framework. One that offers the possibilities for exciting dynamics, not at least when considering the different points of interaction made possible by having layers being influenced by the audience. From picking up a gun and ending another character to entering a god-like state capable of altering the rules of the universes one may ask: why the audience should settle for Virtual Reality when Virtual Superreality is at their fingertips?[1] The layers of the Integrated Story Sphere allow influence at every level of the story experience. Reinventing the audience role from the point of origin and creation to the real-time alteration opens up a new gateway into a whole new evolutionary realm of how stories may come alive through their audiences.

ADVANCING BEYOND THE STORYVERSE INTO THE STORY MULTIVERSE

Going further down the rabbit hole[2] of what storytelling can become, storyverse may exist in a multiverse of storyverses. As a Story Sphere or an Integrated Story Sphere is basically the orb that contains a storyverse, the same scenario applies. Multiple parallel dimensions may exist.

Audience story experience visualised with the Integrated Story Sphere is a combination of everything from the core of the audience – story experience relationship to the context of the audience. Because of all the possible sources for influence from various sources, not just the core audience, the creator cannot ever be in full control of what the audience experience. For example, as touched upon previously, people have different cultures and etiquettes when going to the cinema, and sometimes one group's need for silence and another group's social interaction conflict. For someone to indeed be able to increase control the cinema-going experience, it would need further attention, such as when London's Prince Charles cinema employs 'ninjas' to stamp out audience members' lousy behaviour during screenings,[3] or when mobile phones are sealed before entering the highly immersive Secret Cinema experience in secret locations throughout London.[4]

With interactivity and influence at the core of the design model, complete control is even less likely. One thing is whether someone chose this or that direction in his or her story journey, another is how hard it was to kill the opponent, solve the mystery or find the right path. Add AI to this scenario, and even more versions of individual story experiences will manifest themselves. Not just one for everyone who enters an interactive story, but one for every time someone enters an interactive story, regardless of whether they are a first-time visitor or not. The variations and nuances of the story experience become seemingly endless.

Ultimately, these factors lead to a scenario, where a story experience is designed as a dynamic framework, from which the story, experience, the characters, even world(s) and universes are influenced and sometimes even redesigned by the audience that engages with them. One can argue that every time someone enters an Integrated Story Sphere in its original instance, it will replicate itself to fit that person's particular needs and actions. This represents the opportunity of Story Spheres being created in parallel whenever someone enters the initial framework, spawning parallel or alternative timelines that may then be encountered by other audiences, in the process creating yet another new version of the Integrated Story Sphere. To the audience, it is not a complicated situation; when they play a game or enter a themed attraction, the experience and the memory it creates will not be the same as when they return or when someone else takes the same first steps. But, they do not see, or need to see, every instance created. For the creators, designing for parallel story experiences opens a proverbial and admittedly challenging treasure chest for attracting and retaining audiences. People may have tried the experience once, but will need to come back, because next time, while it may still in some way be the same, it will be different. The reason to return adds to the longevity to the story experience.

> Every time someone enters an Integrated Story Sphere in its original instance, it will replicate itself to fit that person's particular needs and actions.

This phenomenon of parallel, unique Integrated Story Spheres being spawned by audience engagement can be described as the Story Multiverse, and managing it when in full effect is hardly humanly possible. Enter AI and its capabilities that will enable the emergence of creating, managing and setting the direction for – not controlling every detail of – a new generation of audience-centric story experience franchises; all with a potentially unlimited number of individual story experience variations, highly influenced by the audience to the point of co-creation.

There are many new opportunities on the horizon with the emergence of new disciplines and possibilities. To play a part in this particular and very likely future of AI-enhanced storytelling, the creator needs to strongly reconsider his or her role in the design, creation and the setting of direction for new, perhaps even intelligent story experiences.

Story Multiverse.

NOTES

1. Paraphrasing a quote from the late 1990s by concept developer and designer extraordinaire, Jon Gjetting.
2. Reference to Lewis Carroll: Alice in Wonderland (1865)
3. https://www.bbc.com/news/av/entertainment-arts-19622445/cinema-ninjas-to-silence-naughty-film-goers
4. https://www.secretcinema.org

CHAPTER 21

The new roles
of the audience

MULTIPLATFORM AUDIENCES

The mental image many story creators and producers have of their audience is arguably that of a group of people placed in the dark of the cinema, in front of the screen or staring at pages in a book, passively viewing the created content. But, what happens when it is challenged with whether the audience should stay put on 'their' side of the screen, merely consuming what is being presented to them?

With the publication of Google's multi-screen world study in 2012: *The New Multi-Screen World: Understanding Cross Platform Consumer Behavior*,[1] not only did it become evident that using more than one screen simultaneously was widespread, it also marked a change in the role of the audience. People were not entirely focused on, or dedicated to, watching one thing at a time, and creators had to start working with how they could accommodate this change in audience behaviour, even turning it into an advantage.

Shortly after the release of the study, this 'multiverse of screens' mindset was used to develop and introduce new multiplatform concepts like The Design Network,[2] an online platform for interior designers and interior design aficionados with an angle towards furniture fashion. The impactful Google report had quickly accelerated the need for a new understanding of how to use various and multiple screens, as well as bringing about the realisation that the role of the audience was changing.

However, even as brands and marketing addressed the convergence of screens, the audience was already moving forward, towards going beyond the screen to explore the immersive space behind it, as well as challenging what their role was supposed to be.

THE IMPACT OF AUDIENCE INFLUENCE

Compared to a static understanding of the audience, which is more like the cardboard cut-outs mentioned earlier than real people, the attributes of audiences viewed from an Integrated Storytelling perspective are dynamic and in a constant state of flux. Audiences are not only defined by the segmentation by geography, demographics, etc., but also a combination of their overall and immediate role in the audience-story relationship and their momentary modality. Their whereabouts and actions have direct influence on how the story evolves from idea to living experience.

> The attributes of audiences viewed from an Integrated Storytelling perspective are dynamic and in a constant state of flux.

LEVELS OF INFLUENCE

Once past the traditional perception of the audience, they are enabled to influence the story experience, just as it influences them. The different roles of the audience can be defined with a list of increasingly higher levels of influence from passive observer to interacting user to being engaged in co-creation. Every step is a step further towards the story being driven by the audience, rather than being under the control and direction of the creator. It should be mentioned that observation could be just as valuable and enjoyable as interaction or co-creation.

The level of observation

The traditional role of the audience, passively absorbing – and hopefully enjoying – the content the creators present them with.

The level of exploration

Allowing the audience to explore the story world, popular examples being walking through the themed surroundings of a theme park and digital journeys into virtual worlds.

The level of interaction

The audience is interacting with objects and elements found within the story worlds, ranging from knocking over rocks, shooting creatures and interacting with characters on predefined paths and events in video games. Audiences is grated influence on the events, but not the overall narrative.

The level of influence

The audience influences the development of the storyline. Often, clever experience and game design will lead the audience into believing that they do have real influence, even though they are taking one of the predefined routes through the storyline. If this illusion is broken by accident, however, it may spark a backlash from the audience. They may feel cheated, as their apparent freedom has proven to be an illusion.

The level of co-creation

The line between creator and audience becomes more blurred, as the latter influences the creation of the story and its world. Such is the case with multi-player worlds, where the framework of the story allows for the creation of multiple, user-generated storylines and the construction of stages, objects and even characters. Such virtual worlds often co-exist in the same narrative dimension and rule sets as real-world role-play.

The level of creation

At the final level, the border between audience and creator has more or less disappeared, with the original creator now providing the framework for the audience to become creators in their own right. At this point, even the direction of the story is beyond the creator's control, as the audience uses the proverbial story canvas provided to create whatever they see fit.

For this scenario to not be utterly confusing to other audience members, a set of storyworld rules needs to be embedded in the very fabric of the universe of the story. Best-case scenarios: the former creators get to lean back and see what unfolds from the hands of the minds of the audience who are now creators themselves. Worst-case scenarios: the story world itself spins out of control in a parallel to what we sometimes see happening with social media. Nobody knows where things are the way they are, and where they are going, leaving audiences with no option but venting their frustrations.

POINTS OF AUDIENCE INTERACTION AND IMPACT

When combining the nuanced view of the possible roles of the audience with the points of audience impact that are possible in a dynamic narrative design, the outcome is a workable model for defining the aspects of narrative alteration for various types of audience-story relationships.

The Story Sphere provides targeting options for points of impact.

A narrative design model, such as a Story Sphere, makes it possible to break the story components into elements with which the audience can have different levels of influence. It provides points for impact between the audience and the story elements, that to varying degrees like 'knobs' will allow different kinds and levels of influence.

Summarising the Story Sphere, it consists of the following layers.

Universe

The overall framework for the story world, including universal rules akin to gravity, reality and theme. The universal rules for a sci-fi adventure is different from those of a historical drama, as it allows for fictional possibilities such as interstellar travel, alien encounters, etc. The further this comparison, as noted earlier, while flashbacks may be a narrative tool across all genres, some sci-fi universes will allow for characters to literarily travel back and forth in time.

World

This is the world in which our story is set, and should be a complete, rich structure, having depth to its cultures, architectures, landscapes and so on so forth. A well-defined world makes for well-defined inhabitants, which again makes for well-defined characters. Furthermore, a universe can hold several worlds, and each world can actually be a stage in itself.

Space

These are the surroundings where the immediate story scene takes place. It can be inside or outside, and it can be vast or confined. The stage is connected to the storyline; in fact, it does not exist without it.

Objects

Tools, props, weapons and many other kinds of objects have varying importance to the audience-story experience; if you kick a stone across the sand in a western setting, it does not have a profound impact on your story. If you throw the same stone at a lawless gunfighter, it will. Sometimes, objects themselves will have a do-or-die impact on the story experience. Keeping with the western scenario, the key object to the outcome of that particular situation may very well be, whether one has a gun.

Creatures

What makes stories and their worlds truly alluring and relatable is their inhabitants. They are not just sentient, intelligent beings, but can also be animals and mythical and magical creatures that the audience encounter on their journey through the narrative. The scale of intelligence and benevolent or malevolent nature among these creatures can be much differentiated, as their impact on the story. Sometimes, they will help the audience; sometimes, they will hunt them. Sometimes, they will merely add some excitement to an otherwise dull scenario.

Characters

The most powerful connection point between the audience and the story are the characters. The lasting, emotional connection with a story is made between the audience and the characters they can relate to.

Characters take on many forms, sizes and roles within the story, such as hero, villain, friend, helper, love interest, etc., and it is not a set rule that our strongest connection can only be with the good guys. Sometimes, the reason we are both intrigued, entertained and scared by the villain is because we can relate to that person's story as it reflects character flaws or wrong choices that we have, or could have ourselves.

Storylines

When thinking of the audience-story relationship as a designed state, storylines become a series of connected moments, building lines that take us through the action from beginning to end, or on a never-ending journey.

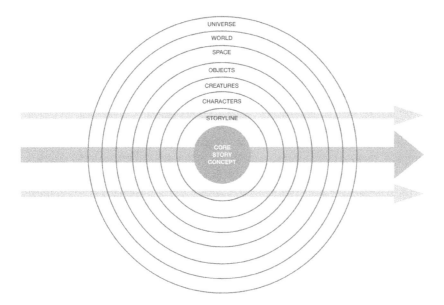

A Story Sphere can have several audience-centric storylines travelling through it.

In traditional storytelling, a creator may work with various storylines such as the main plot and subplots, a combination that is often used to enrich the narrative of television series. Working with the multi-dimensional planes of Integrated Storytelling, those storylines may be alternate routes through the narrative, complimentary transmedia storylines on different platforms, the audience's unique experienced or shared storyline. Dividing storylines into metalines with the rules and chronologies of our universe, main storylines with crucial events in the core story and supporting storylines enables a scenario of choice with which the audience can interact.

COMBINING LEVELS OF INFLUENCE WITH POINTS OF IMPACT

As mentioned above, the most passive audience mode one may think of reading a book or watching a movie at the cinema. Audiences are observant, non-influential of the content they read or watch. On an important note, passive is not to be viewed as a negative role for the audience. Not everything can, or should be, interactive. The possibility for it has been available, applicable and discussed for decades. However, it seems that the need for passive consumption – or rather, enjoyment – will prevail.

> Not everything can, or should be, interactive.

At the opposite end of this spectrum, there are entirely interactive story worlds, created by the audience themselves. In this state, the line between creator and audience is blurred, if not completely removed from the equation. The original author or creator is now more of a provider or a designer of a framework, the proverbial story canvas, for the creator-audience to create and experience their own story.

The latter may sound deceptively alien and advanced, not at least because possibilities such as this are often brought into attention by technical development, that may render the traditional creator-to-audience model obsolete. However, story world-building, as well as story influence through interaction, is rooted deep within us in our childhood. It is persistent in imaginative play, and as play currently is finding its way into the businesses of organisations of our grown-up lives,[3] these types of free-roaming narrative structures may find new life and purpose as well.

> Story world-building, as well as story influence through interaction, is rooted deep within us in our childhood.

Most story experiences accommodate audience roles and nuances that are not at the highest level of influence and the most profound impact of the story-audience relationship all the time. More often, the story experience is built from different levels of influence on specific points of impact. This is not at least caused by the limited time available to a mainstream modern audience to get involved in both the creation and consumption of content.

When applying a combination of audience level of influence with points of impact, key intersections can be mapped into a model like the one below. It defines the design of the audience-story relationship using not every possible level of influence, but those that are most essential to the story experience.

Model for mapping level of influence to points of impact

Level of influence	Point of impact					
	World	Stage	Objects	Creatures	Characters	Storylines
Creation						
Co-Creation						
Influence						

Interaction	
Exploration	
Observation	

Example markings mapping level of influence to points of impact

	Point of impact					
Level of influence	*World*	*Stage*	*Objects*	*Creatures*	*Characters*	*Storylines*
Creation						
Co-Creation						
Influence			X	X		
Interaction					X	
Exploration		X				
Observation	X					X

The story creator and designer may choose and combine a series of locations in the grid, defining how to complete the following starting point 'My audience can (level of influence) with the (point of impact) …', a universal story design rule set for multiple levels of influence can be constructed, such as:

> 'My audience can INFLUENCE the CREATURES and OBJECTS, and they can INTERACT with the CHARACTERS as they EXPLORE the SPACE and OBSERVE the WORLD and the STORYLINE'.

Taking these attributes into consideration defines an overall programmatic to a story, creating a foundation for its design based on different roles of the audience. Furthermore, it provides a tool for designing new story experiences based on traditional material, which was originally intended for an observation-only experience.

NOTES

1. https://www.thinkwithgoogle.com/advertising-channels/mobile-marketing/the-new-multi-screen-world- study
2. www.thedesignnetwork.com
3. Such as **LEGO** Serious **Play**, a facilitation methodology developed at The LEGO Group.

CHAPTER 22

Variations of the alien encounter

AN EXAMPLE OF AUDIENCE INTERACTION AND IMPACT

How would you react if you met a vile-looking alien on the surface of a hostile, alien world?

To illustrate how different points of interaction can influence a story, the example of an alien encounter can be used, such as it would usually unfold in game design or interactive story. In this example, the rules of the universe are maintained as science fiction, and the world in which the scene appears is the generally identified Alien Planet.

The basic, simplified sequence of events is based on a heroine encountering an alien species on the Alien Planet. To alter the sequence outcome, use or non-use of Objects and Characters is applied in a short series of examples with different outcomes.

Sequence 1 (Object)

The alien draws its weapon.

The alien attacks.

The player/audience chooses to have the heroine draw her weapon and counter-attack.

The alien is killed.

Outcome: The heroine is the winning hero over a hostile alien species. In this case, how the audience uses an Object with a Character defines the outcome.

Sequence 2 (Object)

The alien draws its weapon.

The alien attacks.

The player/audience does not have access to a weapon to have the heroine
counter-attack.

The heroine is killed.

Outcome: The heroine is a victim not killed by a hostile alien species.
In this case, how the audience uses an Object with a Character also
defines the outcome.

Sequence 3 (Object and Character)

The alien does not draw its weapon.

The alien does not attack.

The player/audience chooses to have the heroine draw her weapon and attack the alien.

The alien is killed

Outcome: The heroine effectively becomes the aggressor, to the point of having her become the villain, as the alien never attacked, to begin with.

Presented in this limited context, which only describes this one meeting, there is, of course, no past story development to take into consideration. Could this be a revenge or has the alien proven to be a lethal aggressor, as would be the case with the xenomorphs from the Alien franchise. Knowing them and their 'perfect killing machine' behaviour could justify the killing of one, even before it has attacked.

In the specific case of Sequence 3, the alien is being killed without provocation, perhaps even without being armed. It is a scenario that changes the dynamics of the story and flips the roles of the human heroine and the alien villain to the human villain and the alien victim in which the female human represents a hostile, invasive species.

As these sequences show, points of interaction and influence regarding Character and Objects can change the story from being one of the typical science fiction adventures to a tragedy to a cautionary tale reflecting on a history of murders of indigenous people.

CHAPTER 23

From theory to practice: Audience role timeline mapping

We have established that the audience role is changing. Furthermore, the role can be defined as an overall strategy for the general approach to the concept but can also be added as a dynamic to the story experience, shifting from one part of the story to the next.

The traditional three-act structure is directly applicable to spatial and experiential narratives. It mirrors the before, during and after of a design with a lead in and a lead out with the climactic action in-between. Each of the three acts can contain changes and dynamics as well, adding further to the richness of the experience, while keeping in mind the importance of not trying to do having the audience do too much at the same time.

With a visualisation of the story timeline, the shift of the roles from observation to creation can be marked across each of the three acts in order to define a logic, yet surprising and a rich, not overloaded structure from beginning to end.

For each of the acts, define what the audience is supposed to do to move the experience forward. Mark it on the story timeline to visualise the dynamic of the role over time.

- One beginning might be to Observe the instructions or backstory, then start to Explore their surroundings to get things started.
- As you mark each shift in roles, write a short note about what the audience is supposed to do. In the end, you will have a combined visualisation and description of what the story experience is.
- Review it to see if there are anything that should be added or if there is anything that is redundant and should be removed.
- When in doubt, present it as a first-person walkthrough to others, preferably representatives of your chosen audience, to get feedback for further development and design.

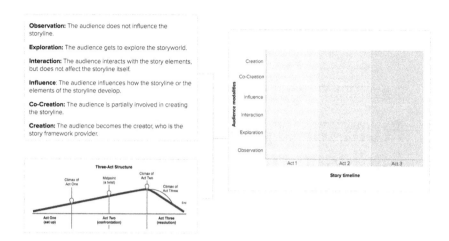

Observation: The audience does not influence the storyline.

Exploration: The audience gets to explore the storyworld.

Interaction: The audience interacts with the story elements, but does not affect the storyline itself.

Influence: The audience influences how the storyline or the elements of the storyline develop.

Co-Creation: The audience is partially involved in creating the storyline.

Creation: The audience becomes the creator, who is the story framework provider.

Audience Role Timeline Map.

Applying modular thinking as used with Modular Storytelling, each of the role marks on the timeline becomes a point that can be altered in order to change the overall story experience, either as a static or dynamic choice. Meaning that the overall structure may stay the same or may be altered due to the audience travelling and interaction with it.

CHAPTER 24

Contextual audience design

Establishing a more diverse view on the modality of the audience is a massive step forward; but still, there is more to understanding and designing for the nuances of audiences. It is necessary to look at the immediate surroundings and situations of the audience; to take a look at the context, in which the audience will engage with the stories.

For storytellers wanting to develop and deliver multidimensional designs, context has various definitions, including.

SPATIAL CONTEXT

• Where is the audience?

The spatial context is in itself a massive universe that can fill more than a whole book, and many brilliant books have been written on this subject.[1] The space that surrounds the audience be it physical, virtual or a hybrid of both, and how it adds value to the story experience, plays an essential part of a story's success with the audience.

TEMPORAL CONTEXT

• When and for how long time is the audience in their current state of story engagement?

Time and temporal context have a substantial influence on the level of storyworld depth and immersion of the audience will be capable of. The audience can be deeply immersed in the story world of a book for hours and hours, which makes space for a wealth of nuances and details. On the other hand, a short social media story or a story-based advertisement, such as an interactive billboard, may only be viewed for seconds. Good news for the storyteller is that when it comes to how good a story is, it is not defined by its length. What is the perfect length of a story? There is no one answer; it depends on context.

SOCIAL CONTEXT

• Is the audience with others or alone?

A lack of understanding of social context can easily prove a pitfall, not at least when adding new, immersive technologies to the story experience. As VR made its return to the mainstream with the Oculus Rift launch in March 2016 and the crowdfunding events that preceded it, it was heralded by many as the new dimension for exploring stories, narratives and content in any context. However, as for attractions, that are mostly visited as a social activity, the code that had, and to some extent, still has, to be cracked was not as much with regards to technology, as it was with regards to making VR social.

As for the state of being alone or being with others when experiencing a story in either audience role, while recognising that people are mostly social creatures, not everything has to be overtly social. This does not only apply to reading a good book in the comfort of your home. Attractions like museums can be just as good an experience on your own or with others.

MODAL CONTEXT

• What mode is the audience in when engaging with the story?

The modality of the audience is basically what people are in the process of doing; what kind of mode they are in. Even over a short time, the audience modality can shift, which can be taken into valuable consideration, not at least for spatial storytelling: theme parks are not just about the ride and shopping malls are not just about purchases. Regarding digital platforms, the tablet or smartphone considered to be the main stage for presenting a game, novel, comic and movie to the audience, can quickly shift into being used for something else. The surrounding or focused modality of the audience is a decisive factor in whether their engagement and immersion in a story or story world are shallow or deep.

One can keep on expanding the list of contextual dimensions. However, many of further additions to the list may be obsolete, as they are mere expansions of the above: Emotional Context may be a given based on the Social Context, Travel Context may be defined within Spatial, Modal and Temporal Context, etc.

To explore the dimensions of audience further, the following pages will be a deeper dive into the modality context, to explore audience modality and to just know how it may make storytelling efforts succeed ... or fail.

THE DIMENSION OF AUDIENCE MODALITY

Revisiting the Google Survey that accelerated the Second Screen and cross-media evolution forward,[2] it introduced the concept of simultaneous viewing and interaction on different platforms to the world of business, quickly adopted by media, marketing and entertainment. Part of this evolution leads to the idea of the continuously multitasking audience, which again was part of the myth of the perpetually multitasking Millennial. People reaching adulthood in the early–twenty-first century who is often portrayed as shallow, superficial and always on social media. Whether the myth will persevere time will tell as many Millennials become parents with responsibilities.

However, fluctuating modalities are even more complicated than merely going from one screen to the next. Understanding the many nuances is arguably key to further evolution of experience and interaction design as well as transmedia design and development. The story experience has evolved from interacting with screen content to the interaction with the story within and the exploration of the space that lies around and beyond the screen. Still, there are even more dimensions of the audience to be explored. People are often in a mode of multi-modality or even hyper-modality, meaning that not only do they engage with more than one thing at a time, what they are doing shifts over time, even with just seconds and minutes apart.

There are a vast number of different uses for a mobile device, and how these uses can shift from one moment to the next. Add to it various kinds of contexts and modalities. Audiences may listen to an audiobook while taking a walk, and suddenly they receive a message and the mode changes. Audiences may play a game on the train while listening to music, to suddenly pause to take a photo or video of a fun or shareable moment, and share it on social media. After sharing, they may return to playing a game or listening to music, but now there is also the luring anticipation whether someone likes or comments on their post. Which then again may initiate a conversation with that someone who engaged with our post. Continuing the game or the story in the audiobook may be put on hold for a while. In the case of some stories, perhaps even indefinitely. Story creators simply cannot ignore how different modalities or even a level of hyper-modalities can influence how their story is experienced.

> Story creators simply cannot ignore how different modalities or even a level of hyper-modalities can influence how their story is experienced.

In his book *Deep Work*, Cal Newport[3] is exploring a phenomenon that relates to creators and audiences alike. Because of the way that people's brains are wired, they can only do a limited number of things to a total depth of concentration at the same time. If a person does five things at the same time, that person can only have a certain level of focus and attention for each of these, and the depth of engagement will be more or less superficial with each of them. If the person is entirely focused on one thing, he or she enters a deeper level of engagement, which, in a *Deep Work* scenario can be solving a problem or writing chapters for a book. It is a state of highly effective, concentrated effort.

The scientific and medical research that Cal Newport references are also useful for the understanding of how the opposing states of focused immersion and hyper modality changes whether our audience experiences our story on a shallow or deep level of immersion and engagement.

The more things people do the less complex each of these things can be. If they are making their way around a hybrid reality adventure, shifting back and forth between exploring and fighting adversaries, they are already using their senses, physical capabilities to capacity, and only have so much left to immerse themselves into a complex narrative. This combination – or overload – of modalities is why overcomplicated storylines that happen simultaneously with physical activity are most likely to fail. Furthermore, the type of modality the immersive, physical adventure presents the audience with, directs their brains even more toward a mode of basic understanding and motor skills.

> Overcomplicated storylines that happen simultaneously with physical activity are most likely to fail.

When the audience gets to focus and concentrate, they are more open to engaging with more challenging and complex narratives. There are digital experiences that have a level of action and interaction that makes gamers frown upon them; they are not considered 'real games'. However, that may not have been the intention of their creators, as interactive books and films have been explored for decades, and can now be distributed on streaming services, such as Netflix's Bandersnatch,[4] an interactive, branched storyline in the Black Mirror series.

It is important to keep in mind that story-based experiences often makes the shift from one level of the modality to the next. The theme park rides have their preshows to set the scene and share instructions, and the video games have their cut-scenes to move the story forward in between the action.

THE DIMENSION OF AUDIENCE ACCESSIBILITY

Young people at the Chailey Heritage Foundation D.R.E.A.M. Centre enjoying the 4D immersive zone in undersea mode.[5]

2nd Chailey Scouts – Chailey Heritage Foundation.

In this chapter, how much influence and context of the audience can have on a story was explored. It was established that the levels of modality define how people can engage with a story experience.

However, one can argue that all of these dimensions are based on deliberate choices by the audience; they decide when and how to connect to our narratives. However, there is a dimension that lies beyond the audience choice and control, and that is the dimension of capabilities and disabilities. It is crucial to consider story

There is a dimension that lies beyond the audience choice and control, and that is the dimension of capabilities and disabilities.

accessibility for the creator, as new ways of exploring and interacting with storylines in various ways also open up new possibilities to audiences that, in many cases, may have somehow been left out. Not by choice but by imposed condition.

For creators of stories and story-based experiences, traditionally, this has rarely been taken into consideration, compared to the world of the interaction and system designers, who often have to take accessibility into account. As the worlds of storytelling and interaction design merge, capabilities, disabilities and accessibility need to become part of the story experience designers' work as well.

> As the worlds of storytelling and interaction design merge, capabilities, disabilities and accessibility need to become part of the story experience designers' work as well.

While not considering technological or reading skills for the following examples, some of the challenges that face parts of the audience, and has to be considered or solved by the creator, are:

- How do the story experience designer create story experiences for those with impaired or no vision?
- How does the story experience designer create story experiences for those with impaired or no hearing?
- How does the story experience designer include those who are in a wheelchair in a spatial setting?
- How does the story experience designer provide alternative means for interaction with people, when speech or hearing capabilities do not allow for a typical way of conversation?

Of course, there are many more scenarios to take into consideration. These are examples, and the point is that the story experience designer should proactively consider any similar scenarios for the particular narrative that is being created.

For some story creators, for whom these concerns are entirely new ground compared to, for example, their well-established capabilities in narrative structures, working to find solutions can be a daunting task. However, the story creator should not look at it with that reservation. It should be viewed as an opportunity to come up with new, innovative ways to include more people in the audience by finding ways to give them access to any given story world. New technology emerges all the time that will allow for the creation of not only Integrated Storytelling, but also inclusive, accessible story experiences.

NOTES

1. Besides the literature list in this book, an updated an extended literature list is available on the companion website. Please refer to the literature list for the link.
2. https://www.thinkwithgoogle.com/advertising-channels/mobile-marketing/the-new-multi-screen-world-study/
3. Cal Newport: Deep Work (Rules for Focused Success in a Distracted World) (2016)
4. Black Mirror: Bandersnatch (Netflix 2018)
5. Image courtesy of 2nd Chailey Scouts – Chailey Heritage Foundation

CHAPTER 25

From theory to practice: Audience context

In summarisation, the context that the audience finds themselves in can be highly influential to their level of engagement with, and experience of, the story. Rather than treating it is a blind angle, the context can be taken into consideration when designing the story and even set the direction for the story experience.

In order to test the influence of the various context parameters, the creator can define the core concept, and then assess how it will be influenced by where the audience is and what they are doing. This is, in fact, taking the step to expand a Story Sphere further than defining the core story concept, and then use the Universe to define the framework for further development. The Context sets the framework that even the Universe unfolds within.

To define and test the context layers and their influence, review them through the following steps:

Core Story Concept: What is the premise of the story?
Core Experience Concept: What is the intended experience?
Audience Role: What is the role of the audience?
Spatial Context: Where is the audience?
Temporal Context: For how long the audience is engaged with the story experience?
Social Context: Is the audience with others or alone?
Modal Context: What is the audience doing when engaging with the story?
Other Considerations: Are there any other contextual parameters to consider?
Review Audience Role: Influenced by context, can the audience fulfil their intended role? If not, what needs to be changed?

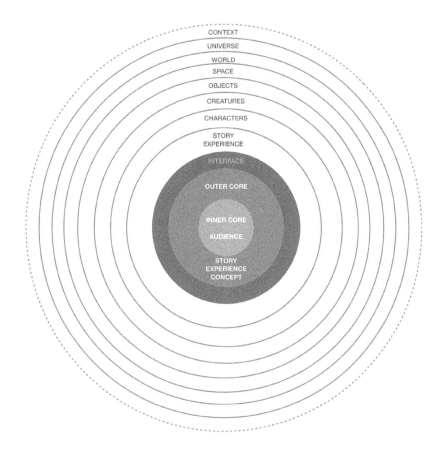

Integrated Story Sphere.

Review Core Experience Concept: Influenced by context, can the experience still be delivered as intended? If not, what needs to be changed?

Review Core Story Concept: Is the story experience played out in context still true to the core story and capable of enhancing it? If not, what needs to be changed?

Overall Review: Is the core story experience concept compatible with the parameters of context, or does it have to be changed to another place, timeframe, surroundings, level of engagement, type of modality or social interaction?

Taking these steps in the early stages of design can ensure that the story experience both fits and plays off the audience context. Not taking them into consideration is opening up your design and creation to a number of considerable, potentially devastating unsuccessful outcomes.

CHAPTER 26

Adjusting to a new audience mindset

Throughout this chapter, the audience has been defined as nuanced, multidimensional characters that are to be rightfully considered as interchangeable, living organisms. They are more than segments and numbers and have even more depth than anything a story creator can define and design in detail. Ultimately, they are capable of shifting their role from audience to story characters to creators in their own right. Thinking of the audience in such a nuanced and rich way gives way for new dimensions of narratives, and story experiences that not only play with surroundings and modalities but also let the audience engage with a narrative, where shifts from immersive, focused observation to a state of hyper-modality influential interaction can happen dynamically.

However, within this richness of options and possibilities, there is also a pitfall that can derail the efforts of the story creator; making things too complicated.

Some of the dynamic, complex dimensions will likely be handled in real time by AI in the future, or as Guy Gadney coined it in Storytelling Beyond the Screen, create 'stories that learn'.[1] In absence of machine learning, however, focus and simplification are the keys to not getting overwhelmed or stuck in a loop while defining the audience in their contexts and modalities.

> Focus and simplification are the keys to not getting overwhelmed or stuck in a loop while defining the audience in their contexts and modalities.

One can boil it down to key considerations, and prioritise what to focus on, just as is the case with the model combining levels of influence and points of impact presented in this chapter. Not every single point in the grid of the narrative and experience design options has the same level of importance for the audience experience. The story creator and designer does not have to activate each and every one of them, as long as the audience is kept at the centre of the universe when designing a story experience. The focus needs to be on what is relevant; not just throwing everything that is available in the mix.

NOTE

1. Klaus Sommer Paulsen et al.: "Storytelling Beyond The Screen" (2019).

Part IV
Experience

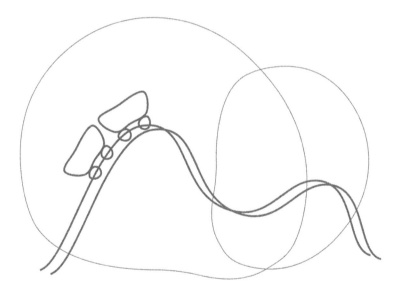

'Tell me and I forget. Teach me and I remember. Involve me and I learn.'

Benjamin Franklin

CHAPTER 27

The design of memories

Experience design with the purpose of enhancing stories, entertainment and immersion – what
could arguably be referenced
as creative experience design –

> The more creative approach is
> the craft of constructing lasting
> memories.

extends beyond practices, as they are known from service design and IT
development. Where the latter is focused on functionality, usability and
applicability, the more creative approach is the craft of constructing lasting
memories that can be encoded with the audience to stay with them in a
multitude of ways. To achieve this, this art of making moments linger
brings together multiple disciplines.

When working with storytelling as a design method, the structures
of the story and the experience mirror one another, which enables both
of them to be built in parallel; as stated earlier, the magic does not necessarily have to begin with the story, and experiences and storytelling have
similar traits. Great storytelling is a sequence of events that become unforgettable storylines. Great experience design is a sequence of moments
that become unforgettable memories. Either of them is a structure made
up of connectable elements; Micro Stories or Micro Experiences that in
combination makes the story become an experience and the experience
a tale worth telling.

MIRRORING OF NARRATIVE STRUCTURES
IN REAL-LIFE EXPERIENCES

With Integrated Storytelling, the intention is to invite the audience into
the story, travel it, interact with it and ultimately, become a part of it. This
journey through the narrative can be established in real-life scenarios,

where narrative structures and steps are more or less consciously brought to life. Think of how the classic Three-Act Structure is mirrored repeatedly as experiences, as the audience dines at restaurants, stays at hotels and go shopping. The dynamics may be more subtle, but from entry point and to exit point – and whatever happens between them – the audience is actually a lead character in the experience that becomes the memory that becomes part of the tale told and retold, often amplified by social media.

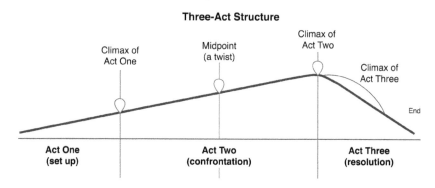

Classic Three-Act Structure.

BRINGING THE CLASSIC THREE-ACT STRUCTURE TO LIFE

Imagine a restaurant visit. Step by step, from learning about it to the recollection of it, the experience is made up of a string of events, encountered by the audience throughout their journey. Events that begin Before the restaurant visit, take place During dining and continue After the meal. A restaurant visit is made up of more than what is on the menu. To the owner and the host, this means that the visit can be designed as a string of moments of positive surprise exceeding expectations that are not only worth living, but also worth sharing with others.

MODULAR EXPERIENCE DESIGN

As is the case with the restaurant example, experiences are not singular entities. They consist of not just one, but multiple events which influence how they are perceived and remembered. This enables us to design them piece by piece, and similar to the Micro Stories, create multiple combinations for the audience to explore. During the dining experience, one may choose pizza, one may choose pasta, and the memory will be somewhat similar, yet different. Also, the pasta may be the better option.

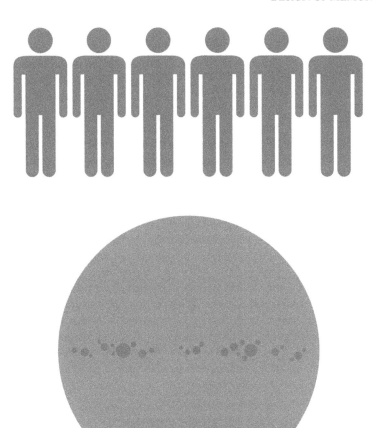

An experience consists of a string of events, or Micro Events.

Each of these Micro Events can be reviewed, edited and rearranged.

Considering experiences as a string of events also makes it possible for the designer to adjust or emphasise specific parts of the event, or micro events, in particular those who leave the audience with a significant negative or positive imprint. Furthermore, it helps avoid event over-clustering. This phenomenon occurs when too many things happen at the same time, confusing the audience and, in the case of live experiences, push the team that are pivotal for bringing things to life too far to deliver on the expectations of the audience. In the reversed situation, too weak and scattered Micro Experiences may result in lack of action and too long period with no events. All of which contributes to the audience getting impatient, bored to the point of exclaiming their aggravation out loud.

Structuring stories and experiences in parallel, modular designs makes it possible to go back and forth between story to experience, and how one is represented as part of the other. When they finally overlap completely, each module becomes more than a micro story or micro experience. It becomes a convergence of the two; what could be designated a micro story experience. As integrated entities, the audience will not have the capability or the interest in telling where either the story or the experience begins at ends. They have become one.

MEMORY TYPES AND MEMORY CODING

When creating experiences, the designer needs to understand and consider the differences between memory types, and understand how they may or may not become encoded to stay with the audience. Even though the ultimate purpose of creative experience design is to establish lasting memories, not every single thing has to be remembered in detail to make an overall, lasting impression. A certain feeling we get from recalling someone, something or somewhere may be made up of many different Micro Experiences, not all of which we remember in particular.

Location-based experiences[1] in these terms are locations with experiences and memories attached to them. What attracts the audience, and what does not, may change due to new technology and the resulting shift in mainstream trends. Consider the movie industry, or rather the cinematic experience. The urge to visit and revisit it was more significant in the time before today's easy access to each and almost any significant moment captured on film from the comfort of our homes. Of course, the cinematic experience is more than the movie itself, but looking at how 'going to the movies' does not evolve to address this, it seems that most cinema owners are even more oblivious to this missed opportunity then their would-be cinemagoers.

In contrast, the theme park industry, having to go there to refresh the memory of it, is part of the sustainability provided by returning guests. They can bring home memorabilia, but never more than memories of the theme park experience itself. The same applies to museums with collections of objects and artefacts. Seeing such pieces of history on a screen does not present the same aura of being in the presence of authentic history passed on through the ages. In an increasingly digitalised world, the theme park and the museum with all their differences and similarities have one particular thing in common: such attractions have to give people a profound reason for making the effort of visiting them, ensuring that the audience appreciated the unique strings of memories in the making that can only truly be experienced on their locations. A string that has to be dynamic to add to the reason for not just going, but for coming back.

> Attractions have to give people a profound reason for making the effort of visiting them.

SIMPLIFIED MEMORY TYPE MODEL

For the purpose of designing memories for Integrated Storytelling, we can divide memories into types and ways of encoding them with the audience in a simple model. It includes a small group of fundamental memory types.

Long-Term Memories: These are the lasting impressions, significant or impressive enough to be imprinted for us, sometimes for a lifetime. The designer has to recognise what they can be, while recognising that the audience does not come as a blank slate. The audience layers can include existing memories that can be used to build from, from fire being hot, water being wet to a particular character of a franchise being a hero or a villain.

Short-Term Memories: These are immediate knowledge that may be discarded when leaving the experience behind. It may the particularities of navigation or functionality, such as where things are and how to use them in the current situation.

Cognitive Memories: These are also considered to be learnings; things that the audience gains an understanding of, an understanding that may outlast the experience itself. Transformative experiences rely heavily on the cognitive triggering of realisation as a discovery of facts – the 'aha moment!' – as understanding strikes. Once understanding is reached, motivation for action may follow, and a step towards learning more has been taken.

Physical Memories: These are remembered, and often recalled, on a physical level. They can include the feeling of getting burnt by a flame, being able to ride a bike or drive a car. For Integrated Storytelling purposes, physical memories are often combined with other elements, as they can strengthen the power of emotion and remembrance. Imagine standing in the forest, smelling the trees and the flowers. Standing at the seaside, feeling the brush of wind and water. Or, standing in a deep cave, feeling the fires from the lava below. Each are imprinted on a physical level through our senses.

Related to the group of memory types, each can be used to imprint – or code – audiences in different ways.

Cognitive Coding: Steps from knowing about something to being able to use the knowledge of it to add perspective. These steps may include

- Awareness of something
- Knowledge of what it does
- Understanding of why it is relevant to someone
- Application of what it does; using it
- Perspectivation in a wider context when adding this new knowledge

Sensory Coding: Ways of using sensory input to create a memory. The senses include

- **Touch** surfaces, fur, pleasant and unpleasant items, etc.
- **Smell** roses, cooking, perfume, pleasant and unpleasant items, etc.
- **Taste** sweets, sour, food, drinks. pleasant and unpleasant items, etc.
- **See** views, persons, objects, art, pleasant and unpleasant items, etc.
- **Hear** noise, ambience, effects, music, voices, pleasant and unpleasant items, etc.

All of which can be combined with each other and other methods of coding memories to increase the longevity of the imprint.

Emotional Coding: Designing to evoke specific emotions and create dynamics through shifts and combination. The number of core emotions can be defined differently, but for the sake of simplified design, the following six basic emotions can be applied.

- Anger
- Disgust
- Fear
- Happiness
- Sadness
- Surprise

Walt Disney is quoted for saying 'For Every Laughter A Tear', referring to opposites that make up a great story. The shift in emotion can be outlined even before the story is defined, basing the narrative of the intended emotions of the audience. With this approach, the emotions can be outlined at specific marks for a story to visualise its intended dynamic and impact on the audience. Deliberately designed shifts in and build-up of emotion can be very powerful, memorable, not to mention great fun.

All of the above are part of a wider understanding of what memories are and how to encode them into the audience. It is a simplified model that enables the story experience designer to make detailed choices in the construction of different types of memories, all of which is part of an Integrated Storytelling design structure.

NOTE

1. LBE: Location-Based Experience

CHAPTER 28

From theory to practice: Micro Experiences in sequence

Working with an event like a restaurant visit visualised in steps makes it possible to add explore what may or may not happen during each micro experience. In the visuals below, the audience journey is marked as a horizontal timeline of events, and a vertical timeline of emotional status; high placement for positivity, low placement for negativity. It should be noted that the higher or the lower placement provides experience designers with clear targets to work from, as what the audience perceives as the best and the worst provides clear points of focus for review and further design development.

The model also applies to other scenarios than that of a restaurant visit, including stays at hotels, shopping and going to the hairdresser – all the memories that become part of the audience's own narrative, and sometimes their self-perception.

To add depth to this model, take the following steps:

- Describe what each step is until critical point of disappointment.
- Describe what the disappointment is, and why it is significant.
- Describe what happens that makes the experience end on a positive note.
- Describe what happens that makes the experience end on a negative note.
- Describe the reactions of the audience for each scenario during the situation and in the time that follows.
- Write two different short stories based on the positive and the negative outcomes from the point of view of the audience. To force you into writing from the audience perspective, use 'We…' or 'I…' rather than describing the events in third person.

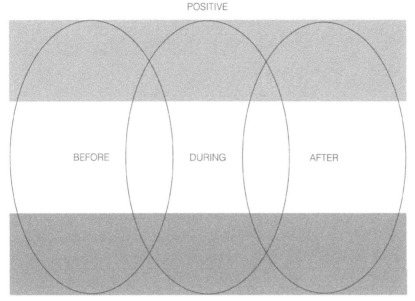

The map of the experience has the Before, During and After on its horizontal axis, and the negative to positive on its vertical axis.

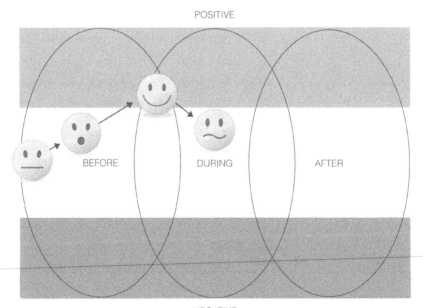

The visitor learns of the experience, decides to visit and is happily surprised when entering; a key experience and confirmation of choice. Then something happens, a disappointment.

POSITIVE

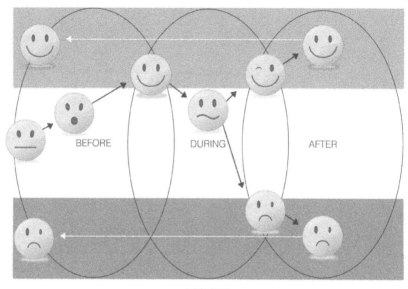

BEFORE   DURING   AFTER

NEGATIVE

The host can choose to explain and remedy the experience, which will turn the disappointment into a story of service and perhaps even understanding of why something happened or is the way it is. Or, the host can choose to ignore or belittle the visitor, creating a story of bad service. Either way, story will be delivered to others, influencing their impression of the host and the experience before they get to make their own impression, all of which is amplified by social media.

What you have just created are actually two comparable experiential narratives describing the audience experience. This memory sequence is the story in which the audience is the main character, or even the hero. It will most likely be shared through word of mouth, social media and perhaps even as a review, influencing whether others will try to relive or avoid the place where this particular string of Micro Experiences took place.

Part V
Convergence

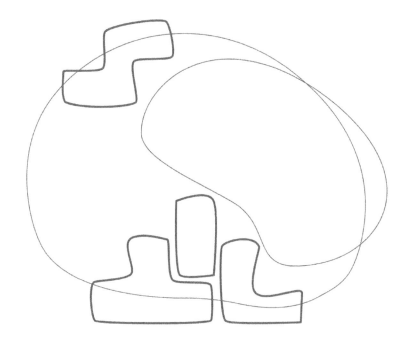

"To put everything in balance is good, to put everything in harmony is better."
Victor Hugo

CHAPTER 29

The Integrated Storytelling design dimensions

When designing narratives for Integrated Storytelling, design goes beyond images, words and sound, even though these are still relevant and implementable in the integrated story experience. With the audience now actively immersing in and participating with the story and its worlds and characters, they become surrounded by a convergence of multiple narrative facets, or what one may call dimensions. These dimensions are not necessarily defined and described by scriptwriters. They can be created by professionals with various backgrounds such as engineers, programmers, placemakers, etc., each of them working to combine disciplines to create a fully developed, interdisciplinary experience.

> With the audience now actively immersing in and participating with the story and its worlds and characters, they become surrounded by a convergence of multiple narrative facets, or what one may call dimensions.

Working with experiential and technical narratives in support of the story and theme are well- established disciplines within the themed entertainment industry. These narratives describe what should happen when, and give consideration to what happens behind the stage, in the proverbial engine room in support thereof. In the dimensions below, the traditional storytelling elements are expanded with new features and possibilities that are all working in parallel, prioritised differently throughput the integrated story experience to be applied as design dimensions as part of an overall design. As such, they are not referred to as various kinds of scripts or storylines, but design parts that can be scripted and storyboarded in individual sequences in adherence with an overall timeline. What the audience experience is the convergence of these dimensions.

The narrative dimensions and design can be marked on a timeline that not only frames the core story experience, but also the events that transpire before and after it.

- For an experiential space such as a theme park, this may be broken down to being at the park, and what happens while waiting in line to the attraction, due to the cue line design and finally, what happens after the ride – such as entering a gift shop or buying merchandise.
- For a cinematic release, going to the movie theatre consists of more than just watching a movie, something that, as mentioned earlier, is still to be explored fully by many movie theatres.

> Regardless of the nature of the story experience, it can be expanded to begin at home, and continue at home.

Regardless of the nature of the story experience, it can be expanded beyond the main site's location, such as a theme park or cinema. Hence, it can begin much earlier at home and then continue at home after the visit. Each of the dimensions below has the capability of making this expansion, even as not all of the narrative dimensions may be applied in full in the final combined story experience design. Once again, when working with complex constructions, focus and priority are pivotal to take the concept from idea to design through development.

STORY DIMENSIONS

The Story Dimensions are found at the core of the Integrated Storytelling experience. They are the stories or storylines that span more than a singular main script to comply with the diversities and variations of storylines made possible with Integrated Storytelling.

Main story narrative design

The main story to build from, with its heroes, villains and what other storytelling elements are needed. The main story can be developed as a core concept or a fully elaborated script, depending on what level of depth that will be presented to the audience.

The purpose of the main story narrative design is to define the main storyline with all the story elements needed.

Supporting story narrative design

In the context of this book, supporting narratives encompass origin stories, backstories, constructed or actual historical events used for world-building and similar narratives that are not necessarily presented explicitly in detail to the audience.

Supporting storylines may also be subplots and other perspectives. Unsolicited supporting storylines may be fan fiction, which, sometimes to the dismay of franchise IP holders and original creators may be appreciated more by other fans than what is considered canon.[1] Particularly for Integrated Storytelling and transmedia, supporting storylines may be individual and interchangeable narratives that exist in worlds and universes where the main story becomes the overall meta-story, framing underlying storylines.

One such case is World War II games that present a fictitious experience with various events and outcomes that make for an individual experience. Meanwhile, the historical meta-story and timeline of World War II persists as a series of events out of the influence of the audience: Events that may span from the invasion of Poland to the bombings of Hiroshima and Nagasaki.

Multi-device representation of multiple storylines makes experiencing them simultaneously possible, as is the case with second-screen use as advanced by Google's 2012 multi-screen world study.[2] Having multiple, supporting streams of content distributed in parallel has been applied to live televisions shows, sports events, games, attractions and more. It is worth considering when it is natural to include multiple devices add more perspectives; layers – or what can perceived as windows into – the story experience, such as when utilising the audience's personal mobile devices.

This story-within-a-story method can be taken to the point of reversing the roles of the main and the supporting storyline, such as when the love story in James Cameron's Titanic becomes the main story with the historical tragedy being the backdrop and secondary storyline. Stories often consist of multiple storylines, sometimes eventually tying them together, to create depth and richness to the narrative. This also applies to Integrated Storytelling.

The purpose of the supporting story narrative design is to define which supporting storylines are needed and what they should contain.

Alternative story narrative design

When a storyline can contain different pathways due to it being interactive or non-linear, multiple storylines and possible endings may appear, in which case, alternative storylines can be explored. This can be achieved in relatively straightforward ways such as having just a few different endings, having the audience chose the hero or the villain perspective, or making choices that open up one or two alternate storylines. However, alternative storylines may also be made up from a long line of choices, ultimately generating new storylines in real time, which may pave the way for AI-enhanced storytelling. The alternative story narrative design is not just scripting alternative storylines, but also making decisions of their structure and complexity and how it can be delivered to the audience.

The purpose of the alternative story narrative design is to define which alternative storylines and endings are needed, their structure and what they should contain.

Audience story narrative design

The audience story is the audience's own account of how they experience something, which they will willingly narrate and share with others. With social media providing just about anybody with a distribution channel, the reach and impact of audience stories have become a factor not to be ignored. Positive or negative stories may almost certainly have a significant effect on brands, services and offerings regardless of industry or market. The impact of the personal account is amplified by the overload of marketing messages throughout media platforms, sometimes disguised as something else. Many find themselves being influenced by what they consider opinions that are more credible and verifications from friends and peers.

Audience stories are much more than reviews on social media platforms, though, as audience choose to share their stories in an increasing number of ways, a trend that is accommodated by sharing stories features on platforms such as Instagram, Facebook, TikTok and whatever next big thing that has made its mark since these words were written.

With easy access to digital video and media tools, new ways of sharing one's stories have been widely adopted, and in particular, YouTube has grown as a platform for individual stories presented as videos since its humble beginnings in 2005. As of 2019, 1.3 billion people use YouTube, 300 hours of video are uploaded every minute and 30 million daily visitors watch almost 5 billion videos every single day. Other ways of creating and sharing audience stories go beyond the established mould for story creation, such as gamers sharing their progress in live streams on Twitch.

Obviously, many brands want to have these audiences interested and engaged while immersed in a brand experience, and strategies and activities to achieve this are developed continuously and deployed. One marketing trend is going from storytelling to storydoing, which basically is to provide the audience with experiences, hints, inspiration and story elements for them to use in their own audience stories across media.

The purpose of the audience story narrative design is to create a framework and suggest a direction for what the audience create and share as their own story.

Interactive story narrative design

The level of interaction and audience influence is part and parcel of the design choices for Integrated Storytelling. As explored in Part III about the audience making their impact on the story, points of interaction and levels of influence need to be defined if the story experience is to be interactive. It is not just a choice of making it interactive or not. It is a design process of making decisions as to how it is interactive.

The interactive story narrative design addresses the interactive elements, how and to what extent they can be interacted with, and how much they influence the story experience. Often, interaction points are objects, but they can also be choices that affect the storyline in which case the interactive story narrative design and the interactive story narrative design may become interinfluential. One choice made by the audience opens up a new pathway through the storytelling, where in turn, a new choice present itself.

The purpose of the interactive story narrative design is to define the level of interaction and audience influence and how it will affect the other narrative designs of storylines.

EXPERIENCE DIMENSIONS

Even though the experience dimensions are presented after the story dimensions here, in Integrated Storytelling, the two act in unison represented as the core of the Integrated Story Sphere, a merging of story and experience. Where the story dimensions are related to the storylines, plots, subplots, etc., the experience dimensions are all part of how the audience experiences the stories brought to life as experiences.

Experiential narrative design

The experiential narrative is a first-person description of how the audience experience unfolds in a step-by-step manner. It is a very effective way to make a story experience concept or design come alive for presentations and testing and can be defined in a script, a storyboard or a video – or a combination of words and images. The experiential narrative can be written as a dramatized first-person account of events, as the designer takes the position of the audience to ensure empathy: 'Then we arrive at the door. From behind it, we hear something growling. We hold our shields and swords tighter as the door slowly starts to open, with the hinges creaking…' rather than 'The audience is waiting to enter the gate. Inside it a beast awaits. They hold their shields and swords tighter, as the door opens'.

The purpose of the experiential narrative design is to define what, exactly, the audience experience is.

Sensory narrative design

Utilising the senses in a sensory design enhances experiences and the imprint of moments as memories. Sights, sounds, smells, taste, touch and feel add to the story experience in combination and utilised at specific points in the story experience storyline. Significant smells at the right time, the taste and impact of sugar, and the physical strain of having to climb from one location to the next are all sensory experiences that can be defined as part of a sensory narrative design. Furthermore, sensory input can be made to recall already encoded memories to add further depth to the experience without using words. Smells of roses, food and brimstone already have specific meanings and values.

The purpose of the sensory narrative design is to define when which senses are to be triggered by what, in alignment with the story and the experience.

Emotional narrative design

Just as the functional and experiential steps can be mapped and laid out in sequence, as mentioned in Part IV, the intended emotions can be mapped out as well when designing a story experience. Anger, surprise, laughter, scares, etc., can be arranged and orchestrated and balanced as an integral part of the story experience. Emotion mapping can also be used as an analytical tool to track and identify the positive and the negative responses from the audience, which can be based on observations by individuals or facial expressions and body language recognition. Questions to be answered through analysis and observations may be whether people seemed bored, confused, frustrated or the more likely intended laughing, exciting or scared when making their way through a haunted house.

The purpose of emotional narrative design is to map the emotions in a sequence as an integrated part of the experience to create balance and dynamics.

Interactive experience narrative design

The interactive experience narrative design is the user experience and interaction design aspects, such as what event occurs when a particular trigger such as a button or switch is interacted with. In IT development, this may also referred to as a use case. Interaction can be based on user input and action, such as pushing a button or firing a weapon, or can be based on user tracking, such as when a light turns on when somebody enters a room. The difference between these is whether the audience knowingly interacts through input actions, or whether the interaction happens without them initiating it knowingly. The interactive experience narrative design can be further developed and elaborated in schematics and flowcharts leading into the designs of interaction sequences, interfaces, etc. It is a valuable asset for the interactive digital design of the Integrated Storytelling project.

The purpose of interactive experience narrative design is to define what kind of specific interaction happens with the audience in the role of users.

CONTEXTUAL DIMENSIONS

The contextual dimensions address the whereabouts of the audience. Their narrative designs may influence main or supporting stories, as these may be influenced by shifting scenarios. Consider time travel as in fiction or when moving from one era to the next in a museum.

Spatial narrative design

The spatial narrative relates to the space in which the audience engages with the story experience, regardless of whether this space is virtual (digital), physical (real) or a hybrid of the two, such as AR,[3] or a combination of VR[4] and physical, such as The VOID.[5]

Spaces can include, but are far from limited to open game worlds, theme parks and themed attractions, museums and cityscapes that all can go beyond creating an immersive framework for the story to conveying stories in their own right. Spaces can tell a story through their arrangement and construction. The above are all more or less obvious choices as immersive spaces with a direct connection to the core story. But to the Integrated Storytelling creator and designer, it is also essential to consider any kind of space when creating audience-centric story experiences.

Spatial settings may include:

- Rooms in the homes of the audience.
- Temporary spaces such as transportation on a bike, a bus, in a car, on a train or a plane, which each have their individual characteristics and related media choices.
- Out-of-home interior spaces such as cinemas, theatres, lecture halls and conference rooms.
- Out-of-home exterior spaces such as guided tours, historical sites and festivals.

For every kind of space, regardless of whether it is directly connected to the story or not in its design, a set of specific audience behaviours and possibilities frames how the best connection is made. There is a difference between reading a book in the quiet comfort of home, physically experiencing a themed experience at a theme park, going on a guided tour with a human guide through a historical site or listening to a podcast while on the road. A transmedia story may create connections from one space to the next, and when it does, the uniqueness of each space needs to be taken into consideration. Furthermore, the space itself may consist of various zones that each has their function or theme, e.g. the lands in a theme park, different exhibition stations within a museum or various levels in a video game.

To the story creator and designer, how each space works, and what kind of stories already exist within it needs to be taken into consideration. Building it may still be part new fiction, but the relevance and often, the authenticity aspect is increased by not ignoring what is already there.

The purpose of spatial narrative design is to take the attributes of a location into consideration to adapt the story experience to specific spaces.

Social narrative design

People are social beings, and audiences are obviously made up of people. More often than not, the Integrated Storytelling experience will have an audience of not one person, but a group of people. Nowadays, a connection is not defined by proximity, so they may not be in the same physical location.

The social narrative design relates to how the audience relates to and interact with one another. A significant part of the story experience may be to collaborate to solve a mystery or get out of an escape room in time. It may include being provided with a natural place to digest and discuss the story or history that was just encountered. Where the interactive experience narrative design defines points of interaction and the interactive story narrative design defines to what extent the audience can influence the story itself, the social narrative design relates to the interaction between the people in the audience. The experience sequence may transpire over a timeframe from the point on non-interaction to team collaboration or contest. Adding even further nuances, the story designer and creator needs to take into consideration that the same kind and level of interaction does not work with everyone. There may people, who would rather be observant as according to the roles of the audience, and cultural differences may dictate what kind of interaction is acceptable.

The purpose of social narrative design is to define how the audience socialises and interact when engaged with the Integrated Storytelling experience.

Temporal narrative design

Stories and story experiences often have a particular timeframe, such as the minutes of the attraction ride, the 20–30-minute television show, the 2-hour feature film, the day at the attraction or the book or game that is engaged with over an extended period, typically not in one stretch. Most story-based experiences that are to be lived from beginning to end without pause have an optimal length of time that will keep the audience interested and engaged with the experience. A guided tour as a podwalk,[6] an escape room mystery, a presentation and a physical contest, all have specific intervals in which they should be delivered based on involvement and concentration needed.

Part of testing a story experience design is testing how its length is perceived to maintain the audience engagement. It may be deemed too long or too short, balanced with what is expected from the audience.

Another level of temporal or timeline design is the possibility of having multiple and parallel timelines. This can be tied in with the alternative story narrative design, in which multiple timelines are defined. Audiences may also have options of entering and exiting a story experience at various points, making for different lengths of story engagement. The parallel timeline can happen in case there are various paths through a story through multiple pathways. This way, the audience may be engaged at different lengths of time; on the other hand, the length may be the same, but what occurs within the timeline differs. The multiplicity of options allows for the story experience design to meet different lengths of engagement appreciated by different audience groups.

As part of the temporal narrative design, there also exists a time context. It refers to the time of day or year, if the story experience is different whether it is explored by day, night, on particular dates or related to a specific season such as Christmas or Halloween. The time of day and season may only be apparent in slight alterations or changes in theming, but the experience may also change completely for a limited time. One such example is the widespread use of Halloween to present an experience that is only available for a limited time, such as Universal Studios Halloween Horror Nights,[7] where the theme parks are transformed from their typical family-friendly environments to a scary environment for the grown-ups. Using popular horror tales as the source for a subtheme that is unique every year, fans are given further reason to return. Each year's experience will be the same, but different.

The purpose of temporal narrative design is to define the optimal length and scheduled time for a story experience.

MECHANICAL DIMENSIONS

The mechanical dimensions are narrative designs of what happens across platforms, media and with supporting technologies. They can be used as a foundation for construction documents, as they describe what the mechanics of the Integrated Storytelling experience are. In other words, the mechanic dimensions is a description of what happens in the engine room to make a concept come alive.

Technical narrative design

The technical narrative is the sequence in which various technologies play their part in the story experience. It is not a fully developed technical requirement document or schematic that is among the documents that will follow for production and implementation. Rather, it is a parallel narrative that supports the story and the experience on a shared timeline with what will need to be deployed and when. The technical narrative design is applicable for multiple purposes, including installations that use technologies in specific places such as attractions, multimedia installations, interactive art, as well as enhanced and hybrid realities. More often than not, it may not be possible for the story designer to define what technology will be needed when. In which case someone with the required expertise can help produce the final document as a briefing for technical specialists to make their recommendations or proposal.

The purpose of the technical narrative design is to define in sequence when and what technologies are part of the story experience.

Platform narrative design

Especially for transmedia and multi-location story experiences, platform design expands from one audience touchpoint to multiple platforms – or multiplatform narrative designs. Platforms are often used to reference a group of social media or other online services. However, in Integrated Storytelling platforms are more than a multitude of screens. They include every relevant touchpoint that provides the audience with the possibility to engage with, and possibly influence, the storyline. This includes, but is far from limited to, interactive installations, cast members, projections, animatronics, theatre performances, XR (Extended Reality), signage, print and sound. If it can provide a meaningful connection to the story, anything can be considered as

> Platforms are more than a multitude of screens. They include every relevant touchpoint that provides the audience with the possibility to engage with, and possibly influence, the storyline.

a platform. The more diverse the platform composition, the more multi-disciplinary skills and teams are necessary for providing specialist services for each platform. To ensure the integration across points of audience engagement and associated specialist skills needed, having someone with interdisciplinary understanding will invaluable to create the connections between each platform and its unique traits.

The purpose of the platform narrative design is to define which platforms are needed when in order to set up a sequence of touchpoints for the audience to encounter and engage with the story experience.

Media narrative design

The media narrative relates somewhat to the platform narrative and what content should be used, when and where it should be used, and in what format it should be delivered. The media narrative design may contain higher-level considerations on what the content may be. However, detailed development, media-specific pre-production and production steps are to be reserved for later in the process.

The media narrative is basically a media plan, including whatever asset should be included regardless of format. It includes taking into consideration which media will have the best effect at a certain point in the storyline, and especially in the case of integrated marketing projects, multiple media may be used simultaneously to accumulate reach and effect.

Furthermore, it may very well be taken into consideration what is realistic, relevant and feasible according to the not only timeline, but the time and space in which the experience will take place. If the temporal narrative design only leaves time for a few, second-long elements and the spatial narrative design, along with the experiential narrative design, makes it evident that the audience is not going to give their full attention to story experience, high-cost production value is not relevant. Short, quick, to-the-point content is.

The purpose of the media narrative design is to define and describe what media content is to be used where and when and in which format throughout the story experience design.

ORGANISATIONAL DIMENSIONS

The organisational dimensions represent the anchoring and integration within the organisation delivering and supporting a story experience to be delivered. Without it, the storylines, audience experience, brand statements, etc., are merely words. Here, it does not matter whether we talk teams and cast members at an attraction, frontline employees in a store, a bank, a travel agent or the actions of the organisation leadership. If the

Integrated Storytelling promise is not the experience delivered, the audience will take notice and leave with disappointment.

Brand narrative design

In the case of Experiential Marketing,[8] the concept stores, brand events and other brand-related activities, the story and the experience need to be in line with the brand represented or brought to life. Ultimately, this will be done in a way that not only adheres to brand visual guidelines but is rooted in the brand's values, background, position, etc.; the brand DNA. Every brand has a narrative, and the brand narrative design can be used to define how the Brand DNA unfolds and expands within the setting of an Integrated Storytelling project.

The purpose of the brand narrative design is to ensure that the story experience is consistent with the brand DNA, builds on the existing narrative and adds further value to it.

Team narrative design

Just like other marketing efforts, a brand story or a brand narrative design does not only have an external audience, e.g. customers and partners. Staff, employees, cast members; the team that makes an organisation comes alive and lives up to its purpose also needs to connect to the story of the brand, take it to heart and, basically, live it. For a team to do so, especially if they are the ones making the brand story come alive with audiences in stores, attractions or other spaces, they need a role in the story. If well executed and well presented, that role can be used by the team beyond the brand spaces and help set a direction for how they represent the company online and on social media. They may have guidelines for online behaviour, but even more important, they have a narrative they play a part in, making it their own story in part or in full, which is much more interesting to share.

In another context, a team narrative design can contain the characterisation for individual cast members in themed settings such as themed restaurants, attractions or cultural heritage sites with actors being present there. This is akin to the live theatre actor's script and character motivation. In themed spaces, the balance tips towards character motivation and insight, giving the cast member some freedom to improvise and act off-script, which is more natural in personal interactions off the stage.

The purpose of the team narrative design is to make the organisation team part of the brand narrative and enable them to make it come alive.

Organisational narrative design

For projects and organisations to run smoothly, a supporting organisational structure is needed, presenting roles and allocating governance and tasks to team members. Often defined as part of a project plan by project leaders and coordinators, the discipline of managing development and operations is a far-reaching group of disciplines outside of the scope of this book.

However, without going into project management and coordination in detail, designing an organisation narrative early in the stage helps define what kind of organisation it will take to make a particular story experience come alive, and anchor representatives from the organisation early in the process. Without their lasting, motivated engagement, the project can be challenged before it's even launched. As is the case with characters in storytelling, the organisational narrative can also be used to define motivations and apprehensions on the part of the team members. When used proactively, the narrative design can also be used to anticipate either the positive or the negative preconceptions and create early buy-in.

The organisational narrative design is basically the story of how the story is made to come alive through people who are presented as named persons or as defined roles. Considering it at an early stage will help avoid developing something intriguing to the audience, but unrealistically to operate. Furthermore, it positively forces the designer to integrate how everything may be handled, once the start button is pushed. After all, it is from that point forward that the Integrated Storytelling design will prove its value to the audience and its creators.

The purpose of the organisational narrative design is to design the motivated team it will take to develop and operate the Integrated Storytelling project.

THE NARRATIVE DESIGN TOOLBOX

With the extensive list that can be built by applying all the narrative design types above, priorities have to be made as part of a clear direction for design, development and production. If the story experience is an interactive book for a mature audience, choices have already been made regarding the spatial narrative design and the social narrative design: the space may not be directly linked to the interactive book, and social interaction may more likely occur after or in-between exploring the interactive story, which will be done by a single person. Change the audience to children or families, and changes may have to be made throughout the various narrative designs. The interactive story may now be experienced by a group of children, parents or kindergarten teachers.

To the story designer and creator, the narrative designs found in the dimensions above are to be considered as a toolbox, and not everything in it should be applied at the same level at the same time. Multi-level experience design may be balance towards being static or dynamic. The balance between the various narrative designs is fixated throughout the experience, such as when going to see a movie, which puts the audience in a rather passive role throughout the experience.

In a more dynamic setting, where the audience is immersed in an engaging the story in a story space such as an escape room or an attraction ride, the narrative designs can change over time, even within a short timeframe.

Entering the first zone of the space, the audience gets presented with the back story and the instructions at which point the level of storytelling is deepest. There may be a shift from introduction to interaction, as a host makes sure that everybody understands the rules and their roles.

A transition is made to take the audience from the first to the second zone, and now the experience starts. At this point, the experience is the priority, and if the story is present, it is simplified in order not to have the audience do too much at the same time. The dynamics may change, as the overall mission (e.g. solve the mystery to get out of the room) may be broken down into a series of smaller missions, each triggered by the completion of the one that is solved before it. In such a structure, the story may be elaborated through the use of Micro Stories introducing new missions may be added. Such narrative connection points are also known as cut-scenes in video game design.

Upon completing the mission (e.g. all the aliens are dead, the door to freedom opens), a more satisfying end to the experience can be achieved by mimicking narrative structures, which does not just end when the main goal is achieved. On the audience's journey back to the real world, their efforts can be celebrated in various ways, such as having a character thank them and let them know that everything is well, and what that means. This also allows for cliffhangers and reasons to come back for more, especially in non-linear story experiences that may hold more than what was experienced. In attractions design, there is often some sort of celebration after exiting the ride, sometimes recalling what was just experienced, such as photos of the audience during the ride. Not surprisingly, the gift shops are often the point of exit, strategically placed when the audience may want to take home a physical memory of their ride experience.

Working with the narrative designs as a toolbox, once the core concept of the core story and core experience have been decided, some of the dimensions may be partly or fully designed. It is possible to review each of the narrative designs individually and decide how important they each are in order to develop, design and present the vision of the core concept. Some may need less focus, and some may even be left out if they are deemed mostly irrelevant. Doing so will ensure that the design work will focus on what is relevant and essential, rather than spending time and resources on that what less importance and impact. All the choices made can be presented in a simplified and unified manner that summarises all the dimensions of Story, Experience, Context, Mechanics and Organisation as a coherent design with a shared timeline. It will showcase what happens on all the narrative strings, as they play out the story experience in harmony on and behind the stage.

NOTES

1. Canon: Part of the official story.
2. https://www.thinkwithgoogle.com/advertising-channels/mobile-marketing/the-new-multi-screen-world-study/
3. AR: Augmented Reality
4. VR: Virtual Reality
5. https://www.thevoid.com
6. Podwalk: Walking tour enhanced by digital media on a mobile device
7. https://www.halloweenhorrornights.com
8. For more about Experiential Marketing, see Part VII.

CHAPTER 30

From theory to practice: Integrated experiential narrative

The experiential narrative is a step-by-step account of the audience experience. It presents the experience as a first-person perspective account of the events that occur, when the narrative dimensions come together to build a personal experience. Where they represent multiple disciplines, the experiential narrative does not take any detail behind the curtain into consideration. Still, describing the story experience as seen and felt by the audience establishes a common understanding, from which each specialist and team member can assess what they need to do to make the vision come true.

When writing an experiential narrative, you will need to put yourself in the place of the audience to tell their story in an empathic and believable manner. A mere second or third-person description of what will happen does not fully convey the impact of the events the audience encounter. Compare the following experience description with the experience narrative:

3rd person description

… Then the audience enters a room with 360-degree projections surrounding them. A soundtrack with sound effects helps the experience become more immersive, as dinosaurs come into sight in the projections …

1st person experience

… Then we enter a dark room. All around us we hear animal noises, leaves rattling and the sounds of something moving around to every side of us. As the light fades in, we realise we are in the middle of a forest. Suddenly, the plants are pushed aside by a giant head approaching is with curiosity. It's a dinosaur!

The experiential narrative incorporates the elements from the narrative dimensions into one, unified experience. Visuals, images, words, spatial and social interaction can be designed and developed in support of it. Note that the empathy with the audience is made by describing both their outer and inner journey in first person. In other words, what happens around them and how they react inside.

To design an integrated experiential narrative that takes narrative dimensions into account, take the following steps:

- Choose four or more narrative dimensions to be combined. This should include the story and the experience, but more should be added.
- Visualise them on a timeline of events, with one narrative design above the other.
- Based on the timeline, write a script of what the audience will experience as an experiential narrative. Leave out details that they will not know of.
- The experiential narrative can be presented in other forms than words; images, sounds, animation, etc., can be added. What is important is that the presentation represents the final experience in a way that invites others into your vision.
- Add or change dimensions to compare how they influence the experiential narrative.

This method is valuable for presentation, testing and evaluation at an early stage. It can provide a concept that has already been scrutinised, perhaps with the help of audience representatives, before further story development and experience design begins.

However, it can also be useful at a later stage. It may be beneficial to explore what changing one narrative dimension may mean to the overall concept before moving forward. Examples of what could trigger changes may include audience test results, relocating the experience or other challenges and opportunities that the project team may encounter.

CHAPTER 31

From theory to practice: Vertical and horizontal integration

The successful design of an Integrated Storytelling structure is built from multiple layers that integrate both horizontally and vertically.

The horizontal integration is the extension a Story Sphere placed on a horizontal plane. It allows the audience to navigate the content of a storyverse and extend the reach of the story across the platforms where its content is based.

The vertical integration is the mechanics and the organisational structure that supports each element of the story experience, often out of sight of the audience. It may be the digital structure of a website that is supported by the governance structure of an integrated marketing team. Layer upon layer, the depth of the vertical integration needs to be defined in order to create an overview of what it takes to establish, maintain and operate the story experience. The audience only engages with the layer

The audience experience is given width and reach by the horizontal integration and depth and, at the same time, support extended by the vertical integration.

they travel, as they engage with the story horizontally, but just as the iceberg, the majority of the structure lies beneath the surface.

To assess what is that is needed horizontally and vertically, ask yourself questions like the following.

Horizontal (the audience perspective)

- What will the audience meet on their journey in the story experience design?
- What platforms are these points of engagements presented with, noting that team and cast members may be considered as platforms?
- What is the brand experience?
- …

Vertical (the creator perspective)

- What needs to be developed and produced for the platforms?
- What is needed for operations and maintenance, including crew and cast members?
- Who supports this project as an extension of the brand experience?
- …

For each horizontal question and answer, a corresponding vertical question and answer will have to be stated. This approach helps building a list that in essence answers what the audience experience and how it is realised by the project team. You may find that some things you do not have the answers for, which is also valuable. Then you will be aware of what you need to find out, rather than moving forward not knowing what you need to know.

Review the questions and answers you have come up with to find if something should be added or removed, and then go back to your list to do so. Once you have the final list outlined, a more detailed working model for project development and related considerations can be developed.

Part VI
Creation

'Well done is better than well said.'

Benjamin Franklin

CHAPTER 32

Creating Integrated Storytelling

IDENTIFYING THE PURPOSE OF THE STORY EXPERIENCE

Storytelling, in its traditional forms, is much more than the discipline of presenting a series of events. The combined dynamics that have made up storytelling experiences for tens of thousands of years are a merges the storyteller, the media, the presentation and the audience. With Integrated Storytelling, even more aspects are added because of the interaction with and influence by the audience, the many different narrative structures available, new ways of distribution of the audience experience and storylines that may not be fully controlled by the storyteller. With these new scenarios, the storytellers have to evolve into story experience designers and story experience creators.

Before the choice of platform, formats and ways of influencing and immersion, the modern story designer has to make the same choice as generations before, i.e. that of defining the purpose of the story.

> The modern story designer has to make the same choice as generations before, i.e. that of defining the purpose of the story.

What is it supposed to achieve and in what context does it exist to accomplish its goal? Without some basic decisions of what the power of storytelling, and especially the power of Integrated Storytelling, is being used for, chances are that the result is merely an exercise in applied technology and methodology and not at least, design principles. One may think that sticking to the formulas, the end result will bring forward a strong message, an emotional connection and physical or psychological immersion, but without purpose, it does not. To the contrary, a connection with the audience may not even be made, as they could react with indifference or confusion.

A shared purpose of a story experience is the point where the connection between the creator's and the audience's wants and needs meets mutual benefit. Successfully formulated before defining the story and the experience, it is the creative strategy that sets the direction for the subsequent development of story and experience from idea to production to publication or launch and beyond. For the story designer to be aware of the purpose and value of a story experience from the point of the creator as well as the point of the audience helps make the right choices to make not just an expression, but also an impression.

A set of universal story purpose strategies can be defined, and choosing one or the other – or a combination – also defines the disciplines needed to fulfil the full potential of the story experience. A common misunderstanding is that a story is a story, and once a person can put pen to paper, he or she can create stories and scripts for any format. However, each of the storytelling strategies below demands different skillsets and insights. A novelist may not be the right person to do an experiential narrative. A cultural heritage expert may be better at sharing historical information than creating a highly emotional storyline. A journalist may not be able to handle the interactions needed for social media. Each of the Integrated Storytelling strategies needs to be handled by the right resources.

BRAND STORYTELLING

Purpose: Showcasing the DNA and values of a brand to create an emotional connection between it and its customers. A common mistake is that of a brand story being used as a marketing message, for showcasing product or service benefits and even call-to-actions as would be the case with advertising copy. The purpose of the brand story, however, is to add more depth to the character of the brand and encourage emotional connections and deeper relationships with customers.

To the audience, searching for brand stories is hardly of interest. However, the value represented by the brand story helps people navigate a multitude of services and offerings, which makes it essential for the brand to present its brand story at the right time and the right moment in the customers' journey. It adds personality and transparency to brand presence.

CULTURAL HERITAGE

Purpose: Sharing knowledge and insight about history and how it connects us. Cultural heritage is often presented in museums and at historical sites, and is balancing historical facts, scholar conclusions with a display of spaces and objects in various kinds of presentation. Creating a connection with visitors and residents alike is imperative for establishing an understanding of who they are and where they come from, and by extension why they do what they do, and how they may react to the future.

To people outside the typical museum audience, the concept of cultural heritage may not be intriguing in itself. But exciting stories and characters are of interest, as well as social experiences with family and friends. This makes the case for the creative development and further integration of storytelling and experience design in cultural heritage settings.

DESTINATION BRANDING

Purpose: Sharing the story of a destination and its residents to add positioning and value to visitors and local communities. With an apparent similarity and often connection to cultural heritage, each destination has its unique characteristics and a wealth of location-based Micro Stories. Characteristics that can be highlighted as parts of the destination brand to represent a unique set of reasons for visitors to visit, new residents to settle and make a living for themselves, and add more depth and connection to existing residents and the place where they live.

To these audiences, this set of reasons to visit or reside is why destination branding holds meaning to them. Making the destination story their story is immensely powerful for creating and anchoring the feeling of connection and belonging.

DOCUMENTARY

Purpose: Narrate reality to provide deeper understanding of or support for a real-life issue, from personal to global perspectives. Documentaries range from sharing knowledge about the mating dances of birds and the stories related to antique furniture to addressing severe and more profound issues like society, race and the environment. It is not as if these issues cannot merge, as showcased by Sir Richard Attenborough's '*Our Planet*' 2019 Netflix series, which merged the nature programme format with environmental issues and warnings in a powerful combination of celebrating the richness of Earth while keeping in mind to take care of that which can be lost. The documentary format presents insight and opinions in order to enlighten its audience, but often also influences the public opinion, which has led documentaries to be banned and criminalised.

To the audience, the search for insight and inspiration combines with a need for entertainment rooted in reality, making presenting stories relevant at multiple levels. Not in a fictitious way, unless the programme is a combination of facts and fiction, but with story structures and elements applied to the content being presented. The final presentation may include dramatization to make the most out of the storytelling elements.

ENTERTAINMENT

Purpose: Regardless of media or platform – movies, games, books, comics and theatre – the purpose of entertainment in its purest form is arguably to provide the audience with an escape from reality and to experience adventures and romances set within genres of constructed realities. However, as is the case with classic science fiction from the 1960s and 1970s in particular, it was often more than a Hero's Journey set in space or alien environments. The stories often carried significant messages about society, the environment and the advancements in technology and weaponry for better or worse.

To the audience, entertainment can be limited-time escapism, while still maintaining relevance and a reflection that creates a connection with the story and the characters. To the story experience designer and creator, it is important to remember, though, when the audience is primarily searching for light entertainment, to not overload the story experience with too much deeper meaning and reflections on the current state of affairs. As discussed earlier in this book, a deeper knowledge about the audience is necessary to guide the direction of what to present to them.

EXPERIENTIAL MARKETING

Purpose: Turning the marketing message into an experience, and in terms of storytelling, letting the audience experience the brand and share their own account. Having the audience experience the message first-hand is a very impactful way of affecting audience perception and intention, as it makes a brand and its values come alive, even if only for a few minutes. Interacting with the brand also makes for another kind of storytelling, in which the brand is not telling the story of itself. Instead, the brand is providing the means for a story through the brand experience. This allows the audience to share their story as it was inspired, but not dictated, by the brand. As an essential part of Experiential Marketing, as the experience unfolds, the distribution of the story or stories it creates has to be accounted for upfront for it to create an impact beyond those who were at the site as the brand experience unfolded.

To the audience, experiences are craved, and sharing the experiences is the part of building personal narratives. Not at least when the experience is unique, which makes those who experience it somewhat unique as well.

GAME DESIGN

Especially for video games, storytelling is evolving beyond connecting scenes of gameplay to adding depth to the experience, balancing the interaction in the game with a deeper connection to and understanding of characters, worlds and conflicts. Even though interactive storylines and story-driven games are not new – one can revisit CD-ROM titles from the 1990s such as MYST – a new interest in adding elaborate world-building and more in-depth character building has made a significant impact on game development in later years. To maintain the balance between game and story, a new discipline of interactive storytelling is arguably being established with new titles more focused on the convergence of story and experience.

To the audience, this convergence means richer experiences spanning different modalities that challenge and stimulate both that of immediate button-pushing physical activities as well as the story reveal and mysteries that prevail for a longer time throughout the game. Regarding the role of the audience, a forced passive role or disruptions in the game design flow is to be avoided, though. It will take an interdisciplinary approach as mentioned above to achieve the rightly balanced convergence in story-driven games and gamified storytelling, and whatever their future combination will become.

GUIDED TOURS

Purpose: Adding more insight, knowledge and connection to places and spaces visited. Guided tours are delivered in various ways, such as being conducted by a person or a mobile app. Whereas, the latter makes it possible for visitors to explore places on their own or in a small private group, when the time is most fitting, the personal guide can quickly adapt and customise a route and react to questions and suggestions.

To the audience, the guided tour provides an extra layer to the experience of a place. Especially when going beyond presenting mere information to sharing the stories and the characters related to a space, the content becomes more relatable and memorable to a wider audience.

HISTORICAL NARRATIVES

Purpose: Presenting history to add perspective and background to current events or the evolution of humanity. History, in this context, is the records of humankind in both modern and older times, and can be defined as a specific category, such as national (e.g. the history of France), places (e.g. the history of the Black Forest in Germany), institutions (e.g. the history of Stanford University), sciences (e.g. the history of astronomy), people (e.g. the history of a native population), etc.

To the audience, historical narratives add origin and evolutionary steps from the past to the future. These narratives meet the curiosity and answer the questions that have come out of personal, professional or educational interest.

INTEGRATED MARKETING

Purpose: Invoking relationship or emotional connection between a brand, product or service and the customers in order to make them make a purchase or other favourable decision benefitting the marketer. Marketing has traditionally been the tradition of pushing messages to motivate customers to buy across different media, often with the promise of bettering people's daily lives or skills through accommodating needs at different levels. As part of this tradition, the approach has been to create a need through advertising. However, with online media and user-generated content becoming ubiquitous since the turn of the Millennium, the number of media platforms expanding brand and marketing messages has oversaturated the market; many city residents are exposed to 5000 brand signals and messages per day. Getting the attention and creating the subsequent desire to buy has become increasingly harder to the marketing departments and agencies. Thus, a much-needed transformation of marketing and advertising to work across disciplines and platforms in an integrated manner is happening in these years.

To the audience, marketing messages encouraging purchases are hardly desirable, and most people have a mental filter that will make them ignore that which is detected as marketing ploys. Furthermore, the marketing regulations in many countries ensure that hidden advertising, such as sponsored articles or product placement in television shows, is marked clearly as marketing material. Paradoxically, the modern consumer uses not only peer reviews and advocacy, but also brand awareness and appreciation to navigate the unfathomable number of products and services offered. Branding is as relevant as ever, and making a brand relevant across customer touch points in other roles than pushing sales is pivotal to its future success.

NEWS SERVICES

Purpose: Presenting current events, often putting them in perspective based on political, cultural or even religious beliefs. Similar to the contemporary evolution of marketing and advertising, news media and journalism has reached a point, where setting new definitions and standards for the overall purpose of presenting news is arguably needed.

News, advertising and politics have always been an inseparable entity, with newspapers covering expenses from ads, effectively having the business of delivering news and marketing grow in tandem. Newspapers also made a political stand, usually gravitating towards either the conservative or liberal, the upper class and the working class points of view. Some of the most reliable news brands have built widespread respect regardless of a political point of view. In the twenty-first century, news media have arguably polarised even more, and the trust to established media has deteriorated. This is partly due to repeatedly being called out for not being trustworthy, as when 'fake news' is invoked repeatedly. Other factors are news and stories that were not adequately researched, or downright copied from other media without any deliberation, have been exposed as being faulty at best. The case may be that the balance between presenting news and selling ads have tipped to the latter, as the struggle for survival as news media intensifies. This influences the news content, applying click-bait principles to get as many clicks as possible, and going for the sensationalistic, often negative news.

However, institutions within journalism are actively working in setting a new positive direction, such as Danish School of Media and Journalism (DMJX)[1] inviting to talks and discussions among news professionals to uncover how news media can define a constructive and progressive role moving forward. All the while, millions now look to late-night shows for their news and an understanding of what they mean. It truly marks a momentous shift in the way audiences find their latest news.

To an alarming part of the audience, news consumption has become very one-sided. Readers have always mostly supported the media that corresponds with their worldviews, but with the increased polarisation of online media, many do not get their worldviews challenged but are stuck with a tunnel-view vision of the world. There is a need, although not necessarily expressed by the audiences for more nuanced, in-depth news. News that will apply storytelling in new and engaging ways, sometimes even capable of changing alienation to empathy. One can only hope.

POLITICAL COMMUNICATIONS

Purpose: To create an emotional connection between politicians, politics and voters to motivate the latter to make a choice in favour of the former. A convincing presentation of a political point of view has always been at the core of politics, since the establishment of the first democracy in Athens in the fifth century BC. The word comes from demos, 'common people' and kratos, 'strength', and compared to the rule of kings and queens, the decisions within a democracy are not empowered by the royalty of individuals but by the united strength by the people. The words the people are presented with can rally the support, not at least when it is time to vote on a cause of action or to have an official elected into office.

The power of storytelling is known and rehearsed well in various political settings. It can be the case of one political figure building a positive narrative around his or her person, with an opponent intent on breaking it down, trying to dig up some dirt on the former. It can be the story of what good will happen if one party rises to power, compared to the bad things that will happen, if the opposing party succeeds. Part of this strategy is often to amplify or evoke common, established and sometimes dystopian fears on part of the voters in the process; 'if they win, you will lose everything'.

A contemporary example of the power of storytelling over the presentation of data was how The Patient Protection and Affordable Care Act; also the Affordable Care Act known by its popular name Obamacare was being pushed by the Barack Obama administration. Initially, the presentations were made up of graphs and visualisation, presenting the statistics that were indeed the rational argument for Obamacare. However, numbers are less relatable, certainly in creating emotional connections. Eventually, the Obama administration changed its way of presenting the message and asking for support by ways of storytelling. Rather than numbers, a glimpse into the lives of those affected profoundly by the available public health care plans – or lack thereof – was presented as small stories of real, kind, hardworking people who had undeservedly been put in harm's way. Arguably, this change in communication strategy finally won over the support needed to establish the Affordable Care Act.

To the audience, navigating the political messages and intentions, especially during a general election in multi-party systems, can be troublesome. Some chose to vote on the party they have always supported, and some chose not to vote at all. Not voting is not necessarily to be seen as disregard of democracy, indifference or ignorance. In a situation where every politician seemingly promises the same, but the history of his or her party is not that of promises kept, some will doubt why they should vote for them, or even vote at all. Many voters crave a clear connection and compelling reason for voting for a political cause, person or party. They expect the politicians live the narrative they sell, building authenticity and trustworthiness over time, not only during times of election.

SOCIAL MEDIA

Social media is not one, but a collection of disciplines, methods and not at least purposes and strategies. Nevertheless, there is one consistent purpose and widespread use of social media, and that is the capability of B2C[2] platforms such as Facebook, Instagram and Twitter, and B2B[3] platforms such as LinkedIn. They enable audiences to share, like or dislike and engage in dialogue and discussion. Actually, in hindsight, one might have considered using the name sharing media rather than social media, and, at the moment, the abbreviation SoMe (so me) really reflects a lot of the social platforms; to many, they are more about the individual than the social aspect.

A common, still present strategy is using the social media platforms as traditional channels of one-way marketing or corporate communication. However, social media are, for better or for worse, a two-way conversation and interaction between creators and audience, audience and audience, and so on in a multitude of simultaneous connection and action points. As far as Integrated Storytelling principles are concerned, the internet simultaneous storylines and interaction points to enable audience influence make Integrated Storytelling a powerful toolbox to design social media frameworks that accommodate levels of interaction and influence.

To the audience, interaction and influence are expected on social media, and the lines between creator and audience become increasingly blurred with users becoming creators in their own right. Enabling them to create, share, comment and interact at predetermined levels is a valuable ingredient in creating and executing a successful social media strategy; a strategy that has to be agile and dynamic because the social media landscape and the popularity of specific platforms are in a constant flux of change.

THEMED ENTERTAINMENT

Purpose: Delivering entertaining experiences based on an overall theme for locations such as theme parks and family entertainment centres. The themed entertainment industry originates in the theme park industry, immersing the visitors in a constructed world based on established or new storylines, in which they can get to live and experience key story elements and environments. Some franchises that have been transformed from story to experience include, but are far from limited to, Disney fairy tales and adventures, Harry Potter, Star Wars and the Marvel universe. The storytelling is applied at various levels at various attractions, and occasionally, the story is left to other audience connection points, as the focus of the theme park may instead be that of transferring the design from a movie or a comic book into three-dimensional reality. As a discipline, themed entertainment is increasingly applied to new kinds of spaces outside the traditional theme park, such as retail and museums.

To the audience, themed entertainment provides deeper immersion in the storyworld the experience is based on, and truly allows them to experience the story or history from within. It is literarily stepping into a StorySphere. Themed entertainment is in a state of evolution, where the universal demand for audience influence, interaction and being deeper immersed in the story is driving new innovations in ride-and-park designs.

URBAN LEGENDS

As a modern version of the classic fairy tale, the urban legend plays with the fears of the modern community with an added supernatural dimension, warning of strangers with ill intent. With the almost unlimited and mostly unregulated array of online media platforms, urban legends have found new ground to breed and spread, birthed by not one, but many fathers and mothers who collectively and not necessarily coordinated builds up urban legends with significant depth. To some, not having an urban legend presented with a transition that clearly marks the shift from reality to fantasy, makes it hard to distinguish fact from fiction.

One notable and infamous urban legend is that of Slenderman, who started as an image and rapidly spread across the internet underground and into the mainstream in the format of a game and a movie. Tragically, the urban myth of Slenderman also managed to make a nightmarish transition from myth to reality. On 31 May 2014, in Waukesha, Wisconsin, two 12-year-old children lured a friend into the woods and stabbed her to near-death in an attempt to appease the fictional character to become his proxies. A tragedy that raises numerous questions about the possible harmful effects of storytelling, not at least when there is no longer one source of origin or specific persons responsible for the negative impact of the creation.

To the audience, the urban legend provides a good scare that is closer to home than that of the traditional horror movie, game or other stories. With its roots in local story and history and possible truths, the allure of the urban legend is whether the horrendous tale may be – even partly – true, whether the antagonist is a murderer, supernatural being, monster, alien – or something else entirely. Luckily, incidents like that of the Slenderman murder is far and few between.

NOTES

1. https://www.dmjx.dk/international/about
2. B2C: Business-To-Consumer
3. B2B: Business-To-Business

CHAPTER 33

Testing Integrated Storytelling concepts

Stories in their various formats are tested in various ways, such as the test audience screening of movies, beta versions of games, and reading and sharing of test book chapters. As there already has been some investment in time and resources to get to these stages, a panel of selected people, often experts, have been involved at earlier stages, such as when:

- The movie has to be green-lighted by a studio representative and approved at various stages leading up to a studio executives screening.
- The game has to be approved as part of the concept and development cycle by various levels of developer or distributor leadership.
- The book has to be approved as a proposal, and then has to be reviewed by editors and peer reviewers at various stages along the way. Providing a peek behind the curtain of this book in a parallel to the breaking of the fourth wall[1] known from movies and comics, it is not just being created by one person, with no influence of others. The final product is delivered with the support of assistants, editors and not at least peer reviewers providing their expert feedback as part of the process.

Many choices at the early creative stages of any concept execution are often made by a group of experts, while the review of a more finalised product, such as a test screening is based on the interpretation of a test audience's response. When developing games, the user and interaction design aspects make it essential to have functional tests with users involved throughout the process. Not only to ensure that the players can figure out how to play the game, but also that the game mechanics actually work. When developing Integrated Storytelling concepts, it is preferable to include the audience as early as possible, as the success of its many aspects will depend on how people perceive and may be interested in immersing themselves in the story experience being developed.

CREATOR BIAS AND BLIND SPOTS

To some creative professionals, arguably earlier in their careers, the reviews and edits and alterations suggested (or demanded) by senior staff members or based on audience testing, may seem limiting, skewing a vision or over-simplifying things. The point is, though, to ensure that the audience has interest or understanding of the creation and what it is supposed to do. If this is lacking, they will not engage with it. The final project may be just as the creator wanted it, but it has no audience other than the design and development team, some friends and family, who are most likely are too polite to be honest; they do not get it either.

The reasons for creative projects getting sidetracked is not necessarily a terrible premise, core concept, story or design, but because of the exclusive, often-hidden knowledge the creator, designer and developer have accumulated as part of the process from early research and concept development. One can unintentionally act and react on that hidden knowledge, creating a blind spot and lack of understanding of confusion on the part of the audience. They do not know what has not been shared with them. This applies to an extensive range of concepts and products being tested at later, rather than earlier, stages in their development life cycle. Examples of setbacks include:

- The audience gets confused about which direction to take in a virtual landscape. They do not have the hidden knowledge of where to go and are not given any clear signs to help them navigate.
- The audience in a presentation does not get the reference to E.T. – The Extraterrestrial – during a presentation on storytelling in a former Soviet Union country. They do not have the hidden knowledge of the story, as they do not know the 1982 movie, as it predates their independence in 1991 with nine years.[2]
- The audience gets confused by how to use a new mobile app, because its interaction design is confusing to them; since they cannot figure out how to use the app, they delete it. They do not have the hidden knowledge of how to get the app to perform as intended, because the design fails to bring the features forward in an immediately understandable way. The designer and developer understand what the app is supposed to do and how to get it working, but that knowledge is not passed on to the app users.

- The audience leaves a movie theatre confused and frustrated about the storyline and the characters; it all does not make any sense to them, and they feel that it was a waste of time and money. They do not have the hidden knowledge that did not make it to the script or into the movie, and that includes character and story development that would have made either more believable, relatable, understandable – and entertaining. Or perhaps, the director's vison was just obscured by studio executives.

There are quite a few examples of stories, not at least in the movie industry, that improved vastly in their director's cut or other later versions, comparing to the cinematic release, which is more or less dictated by the studio. *Once Upon A Time In America* often poses as a particularly grim example. Its cinematic release was cut down in length so much that it became illogical and confusing. However, as movie history includes examples of the director's vision being superior to the first cinematic release as represented in Director's Cut versions, there are less widespread tales of movies being saved by studio guidance and final edits. The original *Star Wars* (later named *A New Hope*, and presented as the fourth instalment in the series) was allegedly a mess before it was cleaned up in editing. Actually, Fox Studios reportedly did not understand what it was all about when they signed the contract; they did so because they held belief in George Lucas.

Storytelling and story experiences share a balance of intrigue and accessibility. As Will Store states in *The Science of Storytelling*,[3] the storyteller has to give enough away to get the audience engaged with the story, but not so much that there is no intrigue or mystery left, making the audience lose their interest again. The balance reflects in how a team of people in various roles and backgrounds come together to create a story experience to ensure that the story experience does not become too obvious with no room for surprises and dynamics, or that knowledge that should be unveiled as part of the story experience does not remain hidden.

When designing story experiences, the balancing act includes both the story, the experience and every narrative dimension that converge to make the Integrated Storytelling design come alive to the audience. Even as this may be a very complex structure as part of the hidden design because of the multiple disciplines and possibilities applied, the experience should not be overcomplicated to the audience. However, as the audience is moving through a sequence of events, gaining more and more knowledge of the story, the experience, and how to navigate with both, the level of simplicity is not static. It is relative to the level of knowledge that the audience has accumulated, and becomes a dynamic concept.

DYNAMIC AUDIENCE ENGAGEMENT AND UNDERSTANDING

In her book, *Game Thinking*, Amy Jo Kim[4] points out how a new company or new product can fail by focusing on a grand vision that ends up unfathomable to customers because there is no clear path from the early stages to that big vision. The point is not to lower the ambition but take the steps needed to get there without losing the audience. Overly complicated or blurred offerings makes them easy to misunderstand and hard to buy into.

The same applies to a story experience at each level of audience engagement, and the golden rule is to keep things simple, yet intriguing. Eradicate what is not needed, and create a strong concept with a strong message to get the attention and interest of the audience.

> The golden rule is to keep things simple, yet intriguing.

One way of doing this is to define a high concept, no more than 25 words that describe what the story experience is. One movie example often used and referenced earlier are the following lines, easily recognisable for many who grew up with the movies of the 1980s that begins with the words 'Lonely Boy Befriends Stranded Alien...'.[5]

Using a High Concept helps define not only movie concepts but also Integrated Storytelling concepts in which the core concept is a convergence of story and experience. Not only does it help present the concept to others than the creators for testing, but it also anchors the creative development to a written definition of what is being created.

Beyond its immediate conveying of what the concept is, some requirements for a High Concept add further definitions to it, which makes it possible to set up a list of key questions that the High Concept should meet within its 25-word limit. Below, they are paired with experience considerations to apply to Integrated Storytelling:

- What is the concept?
- What is the story?
- What is the experience?
- How is it original and unique?
- Why does it have audience appeal?
- Why will it succeed as a ... (ride, comedy, game, movie, etc.)?

If one starts to write a list of bulleted answers, not only will the result be less convincing and inviting to audiences. The 25 words will then soon prove to be an unrealistic limitation. The use of the questions is rather to have directions for what the High Concept pitch needs to contain. It should be noted that there are different opinions regarding in the length of a High Concept, where some argue that it should be one to three sentences long, rather than a count of 25 words, which will add a few extra words. The point is, however, to have a limited, yet compelling description that focuses on the critical points in order immediately achieve interest and understanding, as well as anchoring the creative development and design. As the process moves forward, one may need to revisit and revise the High Concept though, sometimes after the impact of testing with audiences.

As the audiences move forward in their engagement with the story experience, so does their knowledge and understanding, changing their perspective with every event they experience in the story experience sequence. The audience will move from a point of expectation to a point of experience towards a point of reflection. As they move forward, the level of simplicity is seemingly the same to them. In fact, the story and the experience have become more complex, because the audience has transformed from one station to the next, becoming more advanced in their understanding in the process. Understanding this dynamic may also help in selecting audiences for a test; perhaps, they should have a piece of specific knowledge or background, and perhaps they should have none, and little to no briefing before taking part in testing a story experience. If they are involved in sharing their opinions as part of a panel during their progress, the questions and the subsequent answers have to be different from those posed before entering the story experience.

When targeting simplicity as a golden rule, keeping the dynamics above in mind helps take the audience evolution into consideration, and when conducting or facilitating audience testing, create a framework of knowledge needed to be collected through interviews, observations, etc., which takes these dynamics into account. If the exact same person is asked of the level of complexity of the exact same scenario twice, as stated above, answers will typically differ before and after the test session. His or her knowledge and understanding have changed through trial, and possibly, error. If not, there may very well be a fault in the design that needs to be addressed.

TESTING STORYTELLING DESIGN

As the Integrated Storytelling is based on design principles, there are several relevant methods for testing which go further than the test screenings, etc., as mentioned above. As the disciplines in this book combine storytelling and experience design methods, they can be deployed for testing throughout the process from idea to implementation and into operations to test working or drafted versions of story and experience and how they work as a story experience.

Furthermore, modular designs make it possible to test the integrated story experience in a process similar to integrated systems development, in which each feature is tested in its own right, then implemented and then tested as part of an integrated system. This iterative process makes it possible to isolate each module, function for testing, reviews and revisions of the story experience to create a better whole, compared to a significant or complete change needed to be made because the integrated story experience cannot be broken down into its elements. Consider a mobile city tour constructed from micro-stores at multiple locations. One of them may prove unsuccessful due to script, location or the experience. As part of an integrated design, the whole tour does necessarily have to be updated. The issue can be resolved by updating or replacing just one stop on the tour.

The testing principles below can be applied throughout various stages of ideation and development. It is essential to keep in mind to avoid the hidden knowledge problem, such as when testing one module without providing context, in which case, the audience is most likely to be confused from the starting point.

The methods below are a selection focused on involving the audience actively in audience-centric story development through the concept, experience and design phases. They do not include statistical research, marketing research, expert testing, automated and similar ways of testing that do not include the audience directly. However, it should be mentioned that artificial intelligence may very well revolutionise the way that testing is conducted, including how we are currently involving audiences.

Participatory concept review

At the early phases of the overall process, audiences can be involved in testing and setting a direction even at the ideation or conceptual state. The overall concept may be in at a very early stage but still needs to be developed enough to be presentable and be the basis of a constructive discussion. It is essential to revisit the High Concept to define what the story is, and what the experience is at this early point, and provide examples of the experience.

In order to get people involved, presenting moments based as experiential narratives allow to put the audience in the middle of the story experience even though nothing has been developed yet. Similar to developing an experiential narrative, the use of present tense, 'we' and 'you' helps to transport the audience into the early-stage concept. Some background music and example images can be added to help create the scenes. A little showmanship is recommendable to break down barriers and enable a state of suspension of disbelief.

The test audience should be allowed to share their questions, opinions and ideas they have for concept and moment examples they have just been presented with. The creative team needs to keep in mind that the purpose of this test is not to convince the audience that the early-stage concept is excellent, but to test its hypothesis and assumptions and gain valuable feedback.

The feedback collected is of a highly qualitative nature, and as such, should contain interviews and observations as well as questionnaires. The organisation of test facilitators should consist of at least two persons, one that presents the concept and engages in dialogue, and one that notes down both the spoken and the unspoken response to the presentation. If possible, the roles can be divided among three people, so the discussion is not handled by the presenter; the presenter may not be able to be completely unbiased, sometimes even defensive in dialogue with a test audience, and the test audience may be a little less honest because of politeness.

Experiential walkthrough

With the story experience further elaborated in detail, the audience can be walked through it in a step-by-step sequence, even one that mimics the different pathways of a non-linear, interactive branching structure. The presentation of the walkthrough ranges from presenting roughs to illustrate what happens, doing storyboards, multimedia scenarios, doing a spatial walkthrough or even create virtual walkthroughs, all of which of course also depends on the scope and budget of the project. Furthermore, elaborate designs can make the test subjects focus on them rather than the concept.

Regardless of how it is presented, the purpose of the experiential walkthrough is to get feedback on specifically designed sequences, and how they are understood and received by the audience. The experiential walkthrough is a script based on the experiential narrative design, and the feedback from the audiences should be reviewed for changes implemented at the narrative design level.

Testing story experiences have a lot in similar to testing interaction design and user experiences related to IT. However, it is essential not to let the test be overly focused on functionality. In the case of testing an escape room, a ride or a similar experience, part of the testing should also focus on whether the experience is engaging and entertaining. Is it fun? Is it exciting? Is it worth the time and money?

Observation is a vital part of collecting the data needed for evaluating the concept and design. Entry and exit interviews and surveys provide essential data too, but observation provides honest insight into what people actually do and how they interact with objects and others, and often, words differ from actions. On a practical note, it may be tempting to have audiences do a live commentary on their experience as they are doing a walkthrough, but especially if it demands physical activity from the audience, modality and especially hyper-modality needs to be considered. The value of 'talk-out-loud-tests' to test interface designs has been challenged as it adds an unnatural element to the experience, where users have to both do something and narrate their actions at the same time. For testing, a natural state as possible is desirable.

Open pre-production design conversation

Any design element can be presented and tested as a hypothetical question, which provides a way of testing multiple story elements and modules even when the elements in question are defined by aesthetics and emotion, rather than their functionality. A well-developed character, creature, space or world is not just designed as a visual element, but also through its description and purpose in the story experience. With this in mind, a basis for dialogue with users can be established to uncover questions that refer to the intention with a specific design element.

Such questions may include:

- Does the villain represent the intended characteristics?
- Does the hero portray the intended arch type to make the audience decode her or him immediately, if that is the intention?
- Does an alien creature come forward as intended, and not be confused for something else?
- Does the space represent the intended mood?
- Does the castle convey the values of the rulers of the kingdom?
- Does the music add the intended value to the scenarios?
- Do story moments have the expected impact?

To collect accurate and usable data, the dialogue needs to be conducted in the most neutral and unbiased ways possible. If the villainous character must be immediately recognised as a villain, the question cannot be whether 'this villain looks like a villain'.

This kind of design testing can be done as an addition to the experiential walkthrough, taking audiences through a combination of the two, adding more context and depth to either in the process.

CONCEPTUAL, DESIGN AND FUNCTIONAL TESTING COMPARISONS

The three principles above are to be applied at the early stage of developing the concept, story and experience to define the creative platform on which the story experience is fully developed, produced and operated. Tests from this point forward have the purpose of refining and uncovering experience design shortcomings, testing the mechanics of the story experience and whether they work. Towards the end of design and development, the combined experience should be tested at a near-complete stage to remedy any last changes that need to be made. Having audiences involved in testing throughout the Integrated Storytelling project phases ensures that fewer changes have to be made later in the process, where they will be more costly and time-consuming. Including audiences in the concept and design may demand flexibility, but on opening, launch or publication day, it will prove well worth the effort.

NOTES

1. The fourth wall is a performance convention in which an invisible, imagined wall separates actors and their universe from the audience.
2. This reference is based on a true, personal story of an occurrence that happened during an Integrated Storytelling MasterClass I did in Tallinn, Estonia, for the Estonian Marketing Association. Admittedly, I did not do my audience research properly, reminding me of the importance of working actively with the audience layer sphere described in this book.
3. Will Store: The Science of Storytelling (2020)
4. Amy Jo Kim: Game Thinking (2018)
5. E.T. the Extra-Terrestrial (1982)

CHAPTER 34

Acknowledging the dark side of storytelling

One thing seldom addressed in books and papers on storytelling and narrative structures is the potential negative impact of storytelling when ethics are put aside. While some disregard the full capabilities of storytelling in terms of changing opinions and mobilising crowds and see storytelling as a one-dimensional entertaining pastime activity, others know and utilise the same powers for less-than-benevolent purposes.

The tragedy surrounding the Slenderman urban legend mentioned earlier is just one example of what can admittedly dramatically be called the dark side of storytelling and how it can impact lives. To the storytelling professional, knowing both the good and the bad that can come from well-executed storytelling adds an essential perspective to what can be achieved with the craft – not to replicate, but to recognise the manipulative and hostile intentions that are also being applied to the craft. Even as this sometimes happens by accident, without the intention of causing a negative impact they on people and people's lives. With great power comes great responsibility, and with the media and technology enhancements and amplifications of the twenty-first century, the storyteller needs to be very aware of his or her responsibility. For the Integrated Storytelling designer and creator, that notion carries even more weight, as the immersive capabilities and reach of the discipline can influence audience profoundly and maintain a comprehensive and constant reach of them. As discussed earlier, experience design can be used to create very compelling scenarios that elicit a state of transformation, effecting the mindset and forward choices by those who lived the experience.

For the story experience designer and creator, knowing some of the common practices of explicit or subtle manipulation will help avoid doing them by accident, while also help discover and counteract them in storytelling and story experience produced by other creators, emerging on social media and elsewhere. A well-established storytelling skillset can be utilised as an analytical tool to identify and counteract adverse and ultimately harmful content.

Many of the storytelling principles that can be categorised as the dark side of storytelling have been present since long before the current state of media and technology. However, evolution and widespread reach of online media have helped empower and accelerate the distribution of what one may call influential negative content.

Some of the indicators that should call for vigilance include the principles below.

CREATING A VICTIM SCENARIO TO ALIENATE A GROUP OF PEOPLE

In 1915, the movie *The Birth Of A Nation* was released in the U.S. Originally called *The Clansman*, the three-hour movie production was in many ways a landmark in cinema history. However, it was also highly controversial, with black men (many played by white actors adorned in blackface) as unintelligent and sexually aggressive towards white women, and the Ku Klux Klan (KKK) presented as a heroic force. Following the release of the movie, the membership numbers of the KKK soared, effectively making the movie the propaganda that helped rebirth the KKK in the United States. More than a hundred years later, mere allegations of men of colour insulting or assaulting white women can still conjure up a state of mob-rule lynch mentality, now accelerated by attention-hungry media and persons on social media, with neither spending time on adequately researching the details of what has actually transpired before spreading the story – a story that in the end can be proven to be entirely fictitious.

To the story designer and creator, it is crucial to be vigilant whether the story experience has the mechanics of creating a victim scenario that will demand revenge against any particular group or person.

POSITIONING A GROUP, COUNTRY OR GEOGRAPHICAL REGION AS THE ENEMY TO TAKE ATTENTION AWAY FROM CHALLENGES AND PROBLEMS

It is one the oldest trick in the book of the rulers of countries, kingdoms and empires. If the people are not happy with the inner workings managed by the ruling class, distract them or point their growing hostility outward rather than inward. With a clear, external enemy or threat the kings, queens, emperors, prime ministers and presidents can maintain a classic helper or hero position with the population. This practice is still widely used by those in power. Following several incidents where what was deemed definitive evidence of other countries was exposed as less definitive or even not being provable, a healthy scepticism has been rooted within most of the media, political opponents and not at least common people.

To the story designer and creator, looking across multiple layers beyond the obvious can uncover hidden intent and help focus on the real problem, not the symptom or the distraction.

ALTERING THE PERCEPTION OF HISTORICAL FACTS

The winners of war write the history in times of peace, and sometimes the stories are skewed to a worldview of absolute good or absolute evil. However, sometimes history is altered by those who did not win, as is the case with a practice of Rameses II, who ruled the 19th dynasty of Ancient Egypt from 1279 to 1213 BC. Many of the impressive depictions of Rameses overcoming the Hittites at the Battle of Kadesh, which can still be seen in Egypt today, are now widely considered mere propaganda, celebrating a victory that never was. This practice does not only apply to times of war. In times of peace, some will maintain a claim of a victory or a level of a victory there never was, and in tenaciously repeating their claim repeatedly, it will become truth to some, if the claim is not challenged.

To the story designer and creator, making certain having verified content is the only way to know if the story being presented, not at least in a political and newer historical context, is in fact not a rewriting of facts to push a political or religious agenda.

RALLYING AGAINST SOMEONE OR SOMETHING TO CREATE SUPPORT FOR A HIDDEN AGENDA

More often than not, when adversity is built against a specific group of people or a cause they are supporting, someone stands to gain a benefit from negative opinions and actions that will follow. The agenda behind the actions may be to move public opinion in favour of a person or a company or remove and obstacle to grow or maintain power and wealth. The level at which this transpires is one of high stakes and high ambition, as impactful and convincing narratives are distributed across television, movies, books, the press and in ways that fully utilise the transmedia and audience-centric principles of Integrated Storytelling.

To the story designer and creator, it is essential to consider and understand the purpose of the story, and whether it alienates innocent people and makes enemies where there none.

OVERLOADING WITH CONSPIRACY THEORIES TO ESTABLISH A CULTURE OF DISTRUST

The Netflix documentary Behind the Curve (2018) pursuits the reason why an increasing number of people can come to the point of believing that the Earth is flat, when the discovery of it being round dates back to calculations made by the ancient Greeks in the third century BC, and has since been proved with the application of many different sciences across the centuries. Historically, it has not been a consistent mainstream belief, with much knowledge being lost in the dark ages. Scientists and philosophers have suffered ridicule, persecution and prosecution with fatal outcomes for standing up for that which is considered scientific truth and common knowledge today. The documentary presents the path from distrusting lesser issues can lead to a state of belief in something most deem ridiculous. With an increasing number of conspiracy theories, alleged and actual fake news in the so-called post-truth society, a culture of distrust have been established. It has not just paved the way for a desire to be able to differentiate lies from the truth, but also the way towards believing in what most would deem unbelievable. Enter the right opportunist at the right time, and the situation could go from peculiar to perilous.

To the story designer and creator, conspiracy theories offer a lot of great possibilities for entertaining stories. However, it is crucial to frame the story in a way that makes it abundantly clear what is fact and what is fiction, whenever there is a chance of the story being misunderstood and misused to push forward the culture of distrust.

OVERSIMPLIFYING ISSUES OF DISCUSSION AND DISAGREEMENT TO ABSOLUTES

With the longing for simpler times arguably being a widespread sentiment, the promise of living in a world of good and evil, with no grey areas in between, has an almost deceivingly utopian appeal. It is part of why so many escapist adventure stories speak to us with its predominant well-defined groupings of heroes and villains with their own good and bad intentions. In support of their agenda, some public persons and political persons will push the notion that real life is absolutes as well, with few or no nuances worth considering. Some have even won general elections in even well-educated countries pushing this concept. The inherent danger within, of course, is that this mindset leaves no room for understanding those who are or believe differently. People are decimated to either friend or foe.

To the story designer and creator, when presenting the audience with adventures, there is the possibility of presenting them with a world of absolute good or evil, benevolence or malevolence, as the imagined world, characters and crisis are not real. When being presented with a story that is supposed to be perceived as reality, the persons involved and crisis will seem extreme, and sometimes unbelievable, when dealing in absolutes for the real world. This lack of realism can be used to identify and point out the shortcomings of that which poses as truth, but actually, is not.

MAKING PEOPLE FEEL THEY ARE PLAYING A SIGNIFICANT ROLE IN A CAUSE BIGGER THAN THEMSELVES TO OVERPOWER OTHERS

Everybody has a desire to belong and achieve some significance through their actions. Our social and tribal mindset predates civilisations rooted in the early human needs of the safety and comfort in numbers, and in present days awarding of countries the title of the happiest nation on earth, individual freedom and control of one's fate and life is a primary parameter for defining happiness. The propaganda movies such as *Triumph Of The Will*, chronicling the 1934 Nazi Party Congress in Nuremberg, and overwhelming events and rallies held by fascists and tyrannical rulers throughout history are all utilising pride, glory, nationalism on a larger-than-life scale. Part of the purpose is to make the attending audiences feel that they belong to, and sometimes fight for a cause bigger than themselves. Sometimes, the cause may be more significant than the conventional concepts of right or wrong.

The story designer and creator, especially those working in movies and shows, should acknowledge that much of the fascism moviemaking, events and iconographies have already been adapted into contemporary pop culture. The inspiration from *Triumph Of The Will* is clearly visible when the forces of Saruman or the Galactic Empire congregate under their banners in *The Lord Of The Rings* or the *Star Wars* franchise. However, in these depictions, the inspiration is used with a direct link back to the Nazi regime and its arrogant celebration of power, nationalism and contempt for those who are different and seen as lesser beings. The use of the powerful instrumentation of the grand-scale experience becomes problematic when there is no longer a distancing to the beliefs such as celebrated by the Nazi party. In designing grandiose storylines and events, sometimes creators has to be adamant in maintaining a differentiation between the hero and the villain and what is right and wrong. Especially when presenting the content to impressionable minds. This should not be considered a call for censorship, but rather a plea to use common sense and acknowledge responsibility.

CONVINCING PEOPLE THAT THEY HAVE LOST WHAT THEY NEVER HAD TO SOMEONE ELSE

As in many other countries, many grown-ups in my home country Denmark have a nostalgic mental imprint that the summers used to be warmer, and every Christmas was a perfect Yuletide white, with the country covered in snow. Contradictory to this popular notion, which is often mistaken for actual memory, in the twentieth century White Christmas has only occurred nine times. This phenomena of believing that something was better or different than it was is actively being used as part of propaganda to push an agenda of alienating specific groups of people, enforcing the claim that they stole or will steal that which never there in the first place.

To the story designer and creator, portraying the 50s as a fun, musical experience with cool cats and sweet ladies enjoying themselves forever at the ice cream parlour is in the same vein as painting a picture of the lives in the old European kingdoms being nothing but romance and adventure. After all, these unrealistic, and to the vast majority of people living in a chosen period, unachievable, lifestyles, romances and adventures make for better stories than the routines of the workers and the commoners, repeating the same tasks and chores day in and day out.

It is not always criticisable about presenting a time as more alluring to what it actually was. There are many great movies and stories that do so. However, if this imagery of the mind has the added notion that it was taken away not by the change of times; but by some invader with bad intentions, it may signal that the story is not about what was, but an attempt at targeting someone for taking something away nobody ever had anyway.

CONVINCING PEOPLE THAT THE END RESULT JUSTIFIES WHATEVER MEANS NECESSARY

In fictitious tales, unless the character building is of a straightforward structure to the point of being black and white as the principle mentioned above, the well-developed villain has another motivation then simply being mean. He or she has a cause that is pursued relentlessly and fanatically which has brought the antagonist to and beyond the point of believing that goals should be achieved by any means necessary and that those who do not agree are obstacles that need to be obliterated. It is a warped version of achieving a better good for the many or those who deserve it – at the cost of the few, or the undeserving. With regard to any case, personal, political or religious, this kind of single-minded fanaticism is dangerous and with the reach of social media, sadly more and more widespread presented as determination to achieve what is seen as the only solution.

To the story designer and creator, emotions are invoked to create connections between the story and the audience. Feelings and emotions have the power of outshining rational deliberation, and that has helped build relationships between the audience and movie gangsters, hustlers, monsters and others that by all rationale should be considered antagonists, not protagonists or anything in-between the two. Emotions are so powerful that the audience will cheer on when the hero brutally slays the villain, even when the bloodlust becomes all too evident. With feelings controlling decisions, people will allow for human rights of others to be disregarded, give up their own claim for privacy and ultimately, allow for villages, towns, cities and even countries to be destroyed. The warning sign to the story designer and creator is when the causes and the people targeted are no longer of fictitious character, and the narrative acts as a conduit for the encouragement of action, sometimes violent, in the real world.

> Emotions are so powerful that the audience will cheer on when the hero brutally slays the villain, even when the bloodlust becomes all too evident.

The principles and methods above do not make a definite list, but addresses some of the critical examples of the negative influence that is being used as you read these lines. The indicators of the dark side of storytelling can and should be addressed within new story experiences or at public discussions, such as the ongoing dialogue about the role of the press and the impact of social media. The point is that to be able to recognise indicators of the negative impact of storytelling, the story creator has to acknowledge both the constructive and destructive power of one's craftsmanship to avoid using dark side of storytelling inadvertently and to call out those who do it deliberately.

CHAPTER 35

From theory to practice: Uncovering hidden agendas

Storytellers are capable of creating emotion, changing minds and motivating people to take action. The power of the word is greater than the power of the sword, and with great power comes great responsibility. Not just to avoid but to recognise the indicators of the dark side of storytelling. As one builds an understanding of it, and how it is used as a propaganda tool by opportunists – not at least opportunistic leaders craving power – one can recognise how it is used throughout media channels and platforms.

To unlock this perspective and test how the dark side of storytelling may apply, walk through the steps below. You may be surprised how you find other communicators, creators and storytellers than the obvious are using some or all of them for their own gain.

- Choose any story that relates to society or community, it may be political statement or news presented in any form at any platform.
- Does the story create a victim scenario to support or alienate certain persons or groups of people?
- *What could the purpose be for doing so?*
- Does the story position a group of people, country or region as the enemy?
- *What could the purpose be for doing so?*
- Does the story take attention away from challenges and problems that should be dealt with?
- *What could the purpose be for doing so?*
- Does the story alter facts, recent or historical?
- *What could the purpose be for doing so?*
- Does the story rally against someone or something, seemingly to push a hidden agenda?
- *What could the purpose be for doing so?*

- Does the story unsubstantiated claims of conspiracy?
- *What could the purpose be for doing so?*
- Does the story oversimplify issues to absolute statements of good or evil?
- *What could the purpose be for doing so?*
- Does the story make audience feel that they are part of a cause bigger than themselves, the one that calls for overpowering others?
- *What could the purpose be for doing so?*
- Does the story support the nostalgic notion that the audience has lost something they never had to someone or something else?
- *What could the purpose be for doing so?*
- Does the story convince the audience that the end result it presents justifies whatever means necessary?
- *What could the purpose be for doing so?*

This is not a check list; it is certainly not a complete list, and you may find that some of the considerations do not apply. However, as you analyse and write down potential purposes, you may, piece by piece, put together what the story is really about, not just in content, but also in the intended impact through its audience by pushing specific buttons for motivation, mobilisation and them to take action.

Part VII
Application

"The question is not what you look at, but what you see."

Henry David Thoreau

CHAPTER 36

Themed attractions

ATTRACTIONS AND THEMING IN AN INTEGRATED STORYTELLING CONTEXT

Defining an attraction as merely a place with a specific design based on, e.g. feature films or cartoon characters, does not really do the discipline of attraction design credit, and in particular not themed attraction design.

There are various definitions for what an attraction is; the power to attract interest, romantic attraction, etc. However, attraction as space has its unique characteristics, such as:

> 'Something that makes people want to go to a place or do a particular thing'.[1]
> 'Something that attracts or is intended to attract people by appealing to their desires and tastes'.[2]

In the attractions industry, the recurring question is that of what the difference between an amusement park and a theme park actually is. Both have the premise of providing a fun and entertaining leisure space, often with a high degree of appeal to families. The short answer is that even though both places have rides, the theme park is based on a more consistent concept, a story theme that can be applied to tie everything together, including the spaces and the experience beyond the rides.

When the attraction space is based on a coherent concept and idea, it has further depth added to it, as it becomes a themed attraction. The concept of theme has fittingly been described as:

> 'A unifying idea that is a recurrent element'.[3]

Combining the basic definitions above with what a themed attraction space is, regardless of its designation such as theme park, museum or brand space in the context of Integrated Storytelling can be defined as:

> 'A space with a unifying, integrated concept that attracts audiences to experience living stories and moments appealing to their desires and tastes'.

Related to theme parks, this includes an attraction like Disney World in Orlando, Florida, that has the unified concept and a wealth of stories from the Disney franchises integrated at multiple levels, including rides, areas, characters, dining, etc.

Related to museums, this includes a place like Trelleborg Viking Fortress,[4] which is consistent in its use and influences from the Viking area, anchored by a an actual historic Viking fortress on the location. The consistent theme from the smallest to the most prominent items includes the items in the shop, the Viking longhouse and the new exhibition centre 'The Lost Shield', inspired by the Viking shields that is intended to bring story, experience and space together through the collaboration of architects and the movie industry.[5]

It should be noted that the themed attractions spaces are not limited to amusement parks, theme parks and museums. They can also include:[6]

- Restaurants
- Bars
- Casinos
- Resorts
- Shopping Malls
- Lifestyle Stores
- Cruise Ship
- Brand Spaces
- Urban Environments
- Mixed-Use Spaces

One significant development of themed places and attractions in the early-twenty-first century is that new types of places and location are continually added to the list, as the design principles established for the more traditional attractions industry are adapted and transformed to fit new kinds of attractive environments.

THEMED SPACES

With the primary anchoring point for the themed space being a place that is attractive to visit, it is crucial to understand the aspects of space within this context. More than a room framing the audience engaging the story, it is part of the story experience that the audience is immersed in. It has features and functionalities that need to be taken into consideration as a part of the combined story, experience and spatial narrative design.

The story can be the background and inspiration for a themed space, but can also be further integrated with the space and the environment. A Design Story[7] is told in a three-dimensional space and can include architecture, cast members, technology, etc. It allows for the creation of a world that people can relate to, interact with and explore in a combination of disciplines such as storytelling, interaction design, performance and theatre. Using the principles of Design Stories, the traditional story can be translated directly to a physical space, which allows the audience to physically or virtually move through the experience of the story. This translation can also be more metaphorical and less explicit.

When reviewing the overall narrative themes for various kinds of themed spaces, it is evident that the type of space corresponds with a certain type of story, such as the examples below defined by Scott Lukas in the highly recommendable 'The Immersive Worlds Handbook: Designing Theme Parks and Consumer Spaces':

Theme Parks: A place can be a story.
Casinos: Replication of a place, or the replication of a feeling of a space, can be a good story.
Shopping Malls: Has often told the story that an abundance of product variation and availability styles is better. This narrative has arguable been taken over – or even 'hijacked' by a seemingly unlimited number of products on the World Wide Web.
Cruise Ships: Tells the story of travel and transport.
Exhibition Centres: Often based on the unfolding of the history of things, places and cultures.

THEMED SPACE FUNCTIONALITY

With the space being more than a room in which the story and the experience come together, it has a specific part to play in the interaction with the audience, and as such the functionality of the room needs to be defined.[8]

What is the audience supposed to use the space for, and how do they know this?

Spaces have specific uses, and even within a similar overall setting, it may differ significantly. In a retail space, shopping, relaxation areas (dwelling spaces), restaurants and open dining areas. In a museum space, there may be spaces dedicated to the exploration of art that cannot be touched and interactive art that should be touched. As the intended use of the spaces differs, the audience needs some instruction in what they are supposed to do and not to do. An essential part of a ride experience in a theme park is not just the thrill and fun of the ride experience, but also the instructions that precede it.

What kind(s) of social interaction occurs?

Referring to the social narrative design in Part V, there may be social interaction between friends and family or with other audience members, even though people may not be acquainted. It is crucial to keep in mind that people are social creatures, but not all are social in the same way, with different ways of enjoying a movie being a constant source of frustration for some moviegoers. Social interaction in the context of the themed space relates directly to the intended functionality of the space. It can be a discussion facilitated by a curator in a designated space at a museum, a game challenge in an arcade among friends, including everybody who wants to join, or the collaboration and interaction between members of a group that make their way out of an escape room. Exploring the combinations of the social narrative design and the experience design not only ensures that the audience is activated as intended in a place that makes sense, but is also a way to come up with new and innovatively themed experiences.

What kind(s) of private use occurs?

Not every experience, even in an attraction space, is social, as some are individual, also when surrounded by other people. A museum visit, an arcade game, a fitting room changed into a clothing experience are among such places. Theming can stretch into spaces that accommodate functions that are not necessarily part of the reason to visit the themed attraction but are undoubtedly necessary areas, such as the jungle-themed toilets in Tivoli Gardens in Copenhagen, Denmark.

With VR and AR being implemented at various attractions, both add a virtual dimension while arguably limiting the social interaction. For AR to work as a social experience, the limitations of the mobile device screen view ability by more than one person needs to be taken into consideration, something that is even more limited to a group when considering AR glasses. A similar concern regarding VR applies when the audience puts on their helmets. VR is an inherently private experience, so the story experience creator needs to consider how to make things social – also referred to as Social VR. One example is the hybrid reality collaborative and competitive VR experiences presented by The VOID[9] that is implemented for leisure and entertainment in various types of locations, including retail.

When aligning the experiential, technical and social narrative designs, the dynamics can change from the more social to the more private, as long as it makes sense according to the story, e.g. reasons for why the audience should put on helmets at a one point, and why the audience should split up at another. When this logic and alignment does not exist, the story experience may be broken as something such as going on a ride or watching a movie together suddenly gets forced into being private, or, indeed anti-social, despite the audience intention of experiencing something together.

How is the audience supposed to navigate?

Regardless of whether the engagement points of the space that represents the story experience are arranged in a specific linear or free-roaming non-linear order, the audience needs to be properly instructed on what kind of space they are navigating and how to navigate it. Lack of navigating does not only create confusion and gets people lost in a space or a story; it can also disturb other audiences and audience members as too many people in one place creates uncomfortable overcrowding, and ultimately raise safety concerns and even cause a sense of panic. Designing a story experience space has to take into consideration how fast the audience should move throughout an area, how many fits in it and how to make sure they can navigate both under ordinary and extraordinary conditions, the latter taking the need for emergency exits into consideration, and installing them with universally, immediately recognisable signage. Safety and health concerns have increased during the 2020 COVID-19 pandemic, which may have a lasting effect on how spaces are designed to accommodate similar situations and restrictions such as social distancing in the future.

Navigation may differ in the level of instruction, with further introduction in the beginning and immediately recognisable iconographic images placed at various points throughout the exploration of the space. One of the simplest examples of this are the way-finding arrows on the floors of IKEA stores, directing the flow of shoppers. With more complex navigation, such as role-playing or physical games that may send the audience in a different, unintended action, human guides or their mobile device equivalents are other options for monitoring and helping the audience to navigate.

What modality spaces is the audience in, and when?

With spaces that have one or more functionalities that the audience needs to meet or fulfil in one way or another, part of defining the relation between the two is determining what the audience is doing – and when. This may change as their journey takes them from one location to the next, with spaces being divided into zones that can have different functions, themes, modes, etc. For a ride, experiential and spatial narrative designs may be connected with a story narrative design taking them from one part of the space to the next while making it part of the story. The main zones in a typical ride design can usually be broken down into:

Entrance

Presents what the ride is, any critical prerequisites (height requirements, warnings for those prone to motion sickness, doing the ride when pregnant, etc.), practical details such as pricing and sometimes, waiting or show times.

Cue line

The cue from the entrance to the actual attraction may be gruelling and is often the butt of jokes about going to theme parks. Some operators are working on different ways to cut cue line waiting time significantly if not totally with fast passes and new ticketing system functionalities such as time reservations and notifications to visitor that it's their turn. This development has been advanced by the demand for social distancing during the 2020 COVID-19 pandemic.

While the development towards shorter or no cues is ongoing, cue line design is almost an art form in itself, intended to entertain visitors and turn waiting into anticipation. The discipline of cue line design often applies various narrative design principles such as experiential and spatial narrative designs. They present the waiting audience with entertaining elements or things to interact with in the themed environment. Part of the experience of the Harry Potter's Wizarding Worlds rides is walking through the fully immersive cue line designs, brought alive by characters and creatures in physical or projected form.

Pre-show

As the name suggests, this is the show that precedes the main show itself. It is usually based in the last zone before the ride itself, or as a transitional part of taking the final step from reality to fantasy, such as being presented in an elevator before descending into the ride mount zone itself, or in a room before the doors open to the primary experience. Sometimes, the pre-show and the cue line can be integrated. The purpose of the pre-show is to set the scene and the characters as well as explain the mission within a story narrative design. Don't let the alien robot leader have the secret power plug. The house is haunted by the ghost of a bride who was struck by tragedy; enter the rift to another dimension at your own peril.

Loading zone

When there are transportation devices, such as Disney's omni-movers, that will bring the audience through the experience safely seated while being able to spin around to view various perspectives, a zone is dedicated to loading the audience into the vehicles, with cast members controlling the flow, seating and ensuring safety. Entering a cinema or a theatre for a show may be considered as a more passive parallel, where the audience is loaded into their seats. The theme parks often manage to make even this kind of loading an entertaining part of the experience with the team behaving in character with the theme. The loading zone also contains final notifications and warnings, and the possibility to opt out if someone changes their mind in the last moment.

Ride

The ride itself is mostly divided into various sub-zones that define the dynamics of the experience with a few exceptions that arguably are the same functions at the same pace throughout the ride like bumper cars. Typically, just as in a storyline, there are various challenges, events and missions that build up to the final event. A ride can be regarded almost as a physical version of a Hero's Journey or a Three Act Structure.

Unloading zone

After the ride ends, the audience leaves the vehicles and the ride area, assisted by the cast members who are still in control of visitor flow and safety to quickly unload the vehicles and make room for the next audience group.

Exit

The exit immediately recounts and celebrates the ride experience; this is where there will be a celebratory dance zone, group photos on display, and, of course, the gift shop to enable audiences to bring back physical memorabilia of their experience. The exit zone is strategically a very opportune location, as the audience is usually profoundly affected by what they just experienced. This is not only a theme park phenomenon. Museums have gift shops placed at exit routes and some NGOs have stands placed when people are about to exit a natural museum or a ZOO, where the audience awareness of issues of nature and preservation being at a heightened level.

The modality spaces – or zones – apply to a wide range of types of themed spaces, with theme parks and rides being only one kind of experience to utilise them. By using the principles for other disciplines and industries, new and exciting ways to explore spaces can be invented. For the Integrated Storytelling designer, this provides new ways of developing and immersing audiences in story experiences.

NOTES

1. https://www.merriam-webster.com/dictionary/attraction
2. https://www.merriam-webster.com/dictionary/attraction
3. Webster's 1913 Dictionary
4. https://en.natmus.dk/ museums-and-palaces/trelleborg
5. https://en.natmus.dk/ museums-and-palaces/trelleborg
6. As presented in Scott Lukas: The Immersive Worlds Handbook: Designing Theme Parks and Consumer Spaces (2012)
7. Scott Lukas: The Immersive Worlds Handbook: Designing Theme Parks and Consumer Spaces (2012)
8. Somewhat inspired by Scott Lukas: The Immersive Worlds Handbook: Designing Theme Parks and Consumer Spaces (2012)
9. https://www.thevoid.com

CHAPTER 37

CASE: Star Wars Galaxy's Edge

Star Wars Galaxy's Edge was designed to be explored and experienced as if visiting the Black Spire Outpost on the planet Batuu, a new destination within the Star Wars galaxy without pre-existing familiarity with guests such as Tatooine[1] or Hoth would have.[2]

Star Wars Galaxy's Edge differentiates itself from other lands/parts of theme parks in size, immersion and detail. It is the combination of the world and the cast members that make it feel as if the visitor is not at Walt Disney World but actually visits the Black Spire Outpost. Usually, Walt Disney World has designated spaces for characters to do meet-and-greets. However, at Galaxy's Edge the characters roam freely and

Droid DJ at Oga's Cantina on Batuu.

©Star Wars Galaxy's Edge at Walt Disney World.

fit into the overall storyline, staying in character the whole time and by that adding to the feel of actually being at on location on fictional planet Batuu.[3]

It is this feeling of total immersion, the feeling of not being in a theme park but actually transported to a different place, that makes the land unlike anything else in the Disney plethora of theme parks across the world. The place offers open exploration, and the visitor is free to choose their own adventure and interact with them in whichever order they want. The main storyline becomes that of the audience experience, supported by the surrounding space and its elements.

Storytelling and theming elements are woven into the entire presentation of the place, from the taste of the food to the look of the houses to the array of sounds that are to be heard in the background. It is a subliminal form of storytelling going on that impacts the mind subconsciously, immersing the player into the world without them being aware of it, like using crackling energy and hisses of steam sounds, that transport visitors to the outpost.

Furthermore, the way the player is invited to engage with the themed space through building droids or flying the famous Millennium Falcon builds on the audience narrative set within. Each visitor's experience will differ since it is an open space to explore with no set course or storyline to follow and invites the visitor to create his or her own story in the context and immersion of the surrounding Star Wars elements.

A themed area inspired by the Star Wars franchise.

Development began in 2014
Announced: 15 August 2015 by Walt Disney Company Chairman and CEO Bob Iger.
Constructions began: April 2016.
Locations and openings: Disneyland Park at the

Disneyland Resort in Anaheim, California opened on 31 May 2019.
Disney's Hollywood Studios at the Walt Disney World Resort in Orlando, Florida opened on 29 August 2019.

Area: 14 acres at each park, which makes Star Wars Galaxy's Edge the largest single-themed land expansion in Disney Parks history.
Includes: Restaurants, shops, attractions and entertainment.
Development and construction supervision by Walt Disney Imagineering executive Scott Trowbridge.

https://wdwnews.com/releases/star-wars-galaxys-edge-fun-facts/

NOTES

1. Tatooine is introduced in Star Wars: A New Hope (1977)
2. Hoth is introduced in Star Wars: The Empire Strikes Back (1980)
3. https://us.cnn.com/2019/11/27/cnn-underscored/star-wars-galaxys-edge-disney-favorite-things/index.html

CHAPTER 38

Game design and beyond

DESIGNING INTEGRATED GAME AND GAMIFICATION NARRATIVES

Video games have evolved far beyond the teenager bedroom to a ubiquitous, multi-platform industry with players of various ages and nationalities playing interactive games ranging from casual gaming to the professional e-sports players. Gaming has become a professional sports industry in its own right that is continuously on the rise.

GAME THINKING

The principles of game design have been applied to interaction outside of the gaming environments and used, for example, for marketing and training, to drive the audience forward and award them for their achievements. The game design principles are also applicable as 'Game Thinking' to business and product development, as introduced by Amy Joe Kim in her titular book[1] as a discipline that unsurprisingly shares some traits with Design Thinking, both being design-based principles.

The game design principles are also applicable as 'Game Thinking' to business and product development.

In 'Game Thinking', Amy Jo Kim makes one very crucial claim regarding gamification, and how the dynamics of the game are often misunderstood by, for example, marketers. Their focus is often on the points, trophies and bonuses, which, according to Kim, is an extra outcome of the gaming experience, but not its essence. A satisfactory gaming experience is driven forward by character transformation, a parallel to character development, in which a character, controlled by and representing the player, builds up new skills and applies them to move successfully forward in the game. For the gamification experience that applies directly to the audience, now no longer just in control of a reflective character, they have become the character. Relating this dynamic to other immersive experiences with gaming elements, maintaining character development is as essential to the game experience, as it is to successful storytelling.

Integrated Storytelling, which is an audience-centric design discipline, the dynamics with character development and character transformation reflects the dynamics of the convergence of the story and the experience. The audience at the centre of the Integrated Story Sphere is both capable of influencing and being influenced by the story experience, which in this case translates into the gaming experience. It creates a unique dynamic in which neither the story experience, nor the audience are static, but either evolves over time due to their interaction. The story experience design needs to be dynamic as well, which can be accommodated by combined various narrative designs to present multiple pathways through the storylines, which can be achieved with Modular Storytelling. Each micro story or micro experience can have its unique characteristics, proximities and placements in a game story grid within which it may even change dynamically.

GAME GENRES AND MODULAR STORYTELLING

In order to design and integrate story experience for games and gamification, it is imperative to have a more nuanced perspective of what a game is. As is the case with a story not just being a story, a game is not just a game. There are significant variations and differences.

While there are various genres of games, not at least defined for marketing and sales purposes, it is possible to designate a limited number of main groups of genres.

In '*Understanding Video Games*', Simon Egenfeldt Nielsen, Jonas Heide Smith and Susana Pajares Tosca[2] offer a very pragmatic approach in alignment with Amy Jo Kim's character transformation as the defining element of the game experience. They propose a genre system based on a game's criteria for success, which puts video game genres to four types, summarised by Andreas Rauscher in his 2012 paper 'Video Game Genres – Typology'.[3]

Action Games are considered by many to be 'the archetypical video game', because classical arcade games like Pac-Man or Space Invaders are based upon this type of gameplay. Nowadays, the action challenges demanding fast skills and a good perception are often combined with puzzle elements.

Adventure Games are 'characterised by requiring deep thinking and great patience'. Of all basic video game types, this genre has the strongest tendency towards storytelling. The plot is advanced by talking to other characters and solving puzzles.

Strategy Games are 'occupying a space between action and adventure games'.[4] This game type focuses on tactical thinking and well-considered moves. Narrative elements can be restricted to simple background information and visuals are often reduced to window-dressing. Therefore, those games offer a high replay value because of the vast variety of tactics leading to victory.

Process-Oriented Games like The Sims or Sim City could fit the definition of a toy rather than actual games. Think of populating and watching an aquarium as opposed to playing 'chess'.

Whether playing a game in an arcade, a mobile device or a console at home, outside or at an arcade, these four genres work as an overall framework for game experiences such as augmented reality exploration (adventure games, strategy games), game- and technology-enhanced mobile play (action games) and casual play like FarmVille (process-oriented games).

Even though the adventure games may have had the strongest foundation for integrating storytelling, technology advancements, franchise-themed titles and the want for designing something with unique aesthetics and storyverses have pushed how storytelling principles are used across genres and platforms. As the research and development of story integration are continuously being explored and brought forward by new innovations, various ways of implementing or integrating the story can be listed as parts of the story experience designer's considerations regarding how to merge the game and the story narrative to create a combined experience.

Examples include, but are not limited to, the following, which are related to the principles of Modular Storytelling:

- Story entry and instruction, not unlike the preshow and loading zone instructions used for themed attractions.
- Linear storyline cut-scenes that are used to move the storyline forward in story modules intersected between game actions. This is a sequence of story modules in a particular order.
- Non-linear storyline cut-scenes, that has similarities to linear cut-scenes, but accommodate a random or free-roaming journey through the environment. When used for advanced non-linear story design, the cut-scene Micro Stories may be dependent on which modules have preceded them. This scenario combines a series of cut-scenes with Micro Stories that can be travelled in various ways.

- Continuous instruction is part of supporting the transformation of the character, assisting the player in learning functionalities as he or she advances through the fame experience. Rather than mere game device and functionality instructions, this can be designed to fit the storyline. In the narrative, the player is not asked to push buttons on a controller, but to pick up and use a particular item, invoke powers, open gateways, etc.

- Backstory and origin stories add to the richness of storyworlds inhabited by characters and help define why they are as they are, without necessarily having to explain it explicitly to the audience. The world and character development through storytelling is more profound than the visual character design or the looks of spaces and planets. The narrative that builds a character, defines his or her personality and motivation, and adds to his or her credibility and relatability. The narrative of a world not only defines how it is to travel, but what kind of residents live there. It may be a paradise, a jungle, an alien world, a historical scene or a post-apocalyptic dystopia. Once one starts to define this world, and backtrack how it came to be, a line of logic is laid out along with inspiration for what might be encountered here.

- Story exit is the satisfactory send-off from a game in line with the dynamics of The Hero's Journey. Games can have multiple exit points, and it should be considered that some of them are temporary, as many players who leave will come back. New opportunities for the use of story can be considered with game experiences and storylines that do not pause because of one player leaving, such a multi-player or AI-driven game worlds. One option may be a story-like re-entry to quickly bring the player up to speed on what has happened while he or she had left the game. This could utilise advanced functions such as being able to filter out what is immediately relevant and interesting in terms of characters, missions, spaces, etc. One could imagine being met by an AI that recaps what has happened to one's friends, allies and enemies, and what that impact have had on the game.

With further implementation of technological enhancements such as AI of story and game experience development design, one can only begin to fathom the possibilities for the pre-game, in-game and post-game design All of which may include automated updates and even generation of Micro Stories and Micro Experiences seamlessly. The structure of the converged game, story and experience may be a smart story engine, capable of reacting to the individual actions of players. It may be not just stories that learn[5] but rather a new kind of combined story and game engines that learn, anticipate and react. The story and game designers will then have to become elaborate story and game experience framework builders to provide an open and dynamic world to the players. They may establish the rules, but not how the game or its narrative unfolds.

THE ROLES OF THE GAME STORY AUDIENCE

Game design and its evolution beyond the screen has had significant influence to the evolution of the role of the audience, as them being active is inherently part of what game design is. That activity has gone beyond the console and device screens, as immersive gaming environments such as virtual and augmented reality along with hybrid physical/digital spaces have enabled the player to literally step into the game. At the time of putting this in writing, it is arguably still too early to predict whether and how the immersive technologies will fare with a mainstream audience for home and out-of- home entertainment on the long run, even with SONY hitting the 5 million mark of PlayStation VR (PSVR) units sold.[6]

Immersive technologies for gaming are not a new concept, and the trend towards immersive gaming has been seen to be reversed earlier, as some players may prefer some distance to the action on the screen. Furthermore, especially for VR, it is generally recommended against having kids under the age of 12 using VR headsets due to the concern that their eyesight not being fully developed at that age. There is also the issue of motion sickness, which not only applies to 360-degree immersive gaming but also first-person shooters. The effect may be counteracted at hybrid experiences such as VR-enhanced attractions and rides, where the real and the virtual movement is in perfect synchronisation. The ride designers in Europa-Park[7] in Rust, Germany, discovered that people were less prone to motion-sickness due to VR if they were on a physical ride, which had its movements replicated in exact detail into the virtual experience.

Revisiting the previously defined levels of audience influence, direct relations to the story within or created by a game experience can be made:

The Level of Observation may not be a continuous audience mode but applies when presenting story modules such as entries, cut-scenes and exits. At this point, the balance of the experience often tips in favour of the experience.

The Level of Exploration relates to both action and adventure genres open-world gaming and when looking for items and clues regardless of genre. Furthermore, part of the process of building objects and spaces in process-oriented games is the satisfaction of being able to explore one's own creation.

The Level of Interaction is at the core of every game, and the level of the pace of interactivity is often tied into the genre, such as the speed of action game and the time limits of strategy games.

The Level of Influence on the story in gaming is often limited to having a few narrative pathways to choose from, while the game interaction may move the game forward or bring it to an abrupt ending.

The Level of Co-Creation in gaming terms relates to the process-oriented and the strategy games as the player being able to create something within a defined framework. In terms of storytelling, the story is often account of the player's experience within the game. Interestingly, this retelling of the game experience on video and via live streaming via channels such as Twitch[8] has become a popular way for others to experience a game as passive observers – if one disregards comments, likes and dislikes as story interaction.

The Level of Creation demands more of the audience compared to The Level of Co-Creation, even with the creative tools readily provided. Still, sandbox games like Minecraft has proven successful in providing a platform for creating spaces and creating games – hence the designation sandbox game. Minecraft may herald a mainstream development in which gamers become creators of their own games, as was the case with the gaming community in the 1980s. This development may very likely affect that of story design, with proper sandbox tools also being provided for the audiences who choose to create unique and original story designs for their personally developed game titles.

NOTES

1. Amy Jo Kim: Game Thinking (2018)
2. Simon Egenfeldt Nielsen, Jonas Heide Smith, and Susana Pajares Tosca: Understanding Video Games (2008)
3. https://www.academia.edu/10376283/Video_Game_Genres_-_Typology
4. https://www.academia.edu/10376283/Video_Game_Genres_-_Typology
5. Klaus Sommer Paulsen et al.: Storytelling Beyond The Screen (2019)
6. https://uploadvr.com/psvr-sales-analysis/
7. https://www.europapark.de/en
8. https://www.twitch.tv/

CHAPTER 39

CASE: The Last of Us

The Last of Us is a genre-defining experience blending survival and action elements to tell a character-driven story about a population decimated by a modern plague.[1]

It touches upon numerous themes like the human desire to survive and what happens to humankind when institutions for civilisation collapse. Similar to other post-apocalypse tales, it revolves around the question 'Who is worse? The humans or the infected?'[2]

The Last of Us stands out from other post-apocalyptic zombie games by painting a realistic picture of a cruel and macabre world, dark, gritty and infected with zombies, with hard choices that the characters and the players have to make in order to survive. Its ability to invoke raw emotions through skilful storytelling, which makes one care deeply about the characters and their moral dilemmas, makes it stand out from any other AAA-post-apocalyptic game that has been released previously.[3]

The games approach is to focus on the world, the storyverse, the characters and the storytelling and using the gameplay mechanics to enhance this experience. The acts of dying and killing are displayed in the cruellest ways possible, making the player genuinely feel bad and invoke the feeling that both killing and dying are to be avoided at all cost. The unavoidable kills in the game make the player feel awful, not just as a player, but also as a person. That ability to engage the player to the extent that those feelings become genuine and the fact that the game is not afraid to become a game that at some point 'is not fun to play' because of these feelings is unique to The Last of Us, making it stand out from similar games within the genre.[4]

The game's approach is to focus on the world, its characters and the storytelling and uses the gameplay mechanics to enhance this experience. The mechanics and gameplay support the storytelling and invoke feelings that the player share with the characters, creating a strong connection between the two. The game storyline displays human mistakes, doubts and resonates with the players, and the father-daughter like relationship between the characters awakens emotions.

Player expression and agency may be limited, but the achievement of intimacy and self-reflection concerning the characters' moral dilemmas through different layers of storytelling will leave a significant impact on its audience. It reaches its narrative goals through the player's experience of being immersed in, and taking part of, a rich, intimate storyverse.

The Last of Us is a 2013 action-adventure survival video game, played from a third-person perceptive.

Development began in 2009 and was kept secret for two years.
Announced on 10 December 2011, at the Spike Video Game Awards.
Developer: Naughty Dog
Published by Sony Computer Entertainment
Sold 1.3 million units in the first week, and 17 million by April 2018.
The sequel: The Last of Up Part II was released in June 2020.
Game director: Bruce Straley
Creative director: Neil Druckmann

NOTES

1. https:// www.playstation.com/en-us/games/the-last-of-us-ps3/
2. https://www.ign.com/wikis/the-last-of-us/Themes#Themes
3. https://www.vice.com/en_uk/article/av9yv4/why-the-last-of-us-was-the-greatest-game-of-the-last-console-generation-450
4. https://www.polygon.com/2013/6/5/4396286/the-last-of-us-review

CHAPTER 40

CASE: EVE Online: True Stories

EVE: True Stories[1] is a unique graphic novel based on actual events that occurred in the game EVE Online, a massive multiplayer online role-playing game set in space 20,000 years in the future. The stories are inspired by player-driven events within the universe, submitted by players, who also commented and voted on them to finally have a few chosen ones presented to writer Daniel Way. Finally, the story Band of Brothers, an event that thousands of players participated in, was chosen and made into a comic book. The 10,000+ EVE online players, that in various degrees were part of the chosen story, are also clearly part of the target audience.

With EVE: True Stories, the audience got to be part of creating a graphic novel by contributing with a version of their own, real-life

EVE Online.

© 2020 CCP ehf.

experiences within the EVE Online game and universe. They were given a platform to tell their own story, giving them a sense of agency and freedom to pick whichever story they deemed worth telling. This way, the audience does not just become the focal point of the story, but also part of the process from beginning to end, as they take place as both authors, main characters and audience.

The approach taken with the creation of EVE: True Stories is a good representation of placing the audience at the centre of attention by the developers of the EVE Online game. The game itself has become a place where players are rulers of the realm with developers taking the supporting role and giving them what they need to develop the space and the narrative as they see fit. The storytelling around the game evolves with the players and their stories and instead of rejecting and reclaiming their control developers have accepted this dynamic, creating a unique virtual and fictional space that belongs to the players.

In terms of the plot format of the comic book, it is non-linear and did not follow the traditional format of having a beginning, middle and end. It is told through multiple flashbacks leading up to the main battle of the story. The narrative is presented through the main character, Haargoth Agamar, who is familiar to EVE players.

Reviews by readers have shown that the plot was written in a way that presumes the reader is familiar with the universe, making it difficult to follow for those with no knowledge of EVE Online.[2] However, the general concept of 'true-life' events that happened in a video game being retold through a comic book story was received well.

A graphic novel based on true events that occurred in the game EVE: Online.

Announced at EVE Fanfest 25–27 April 2013
First book release 19 February 2014
Four issues in total, released every two weeks until 2 April 2014
Writer: Daniel Way (All 4 Chapters)

Artist, Cover Art
Ch. 1: Tomm Coker, David Palumbo
Ch. 2: Alejandro Aragón, Jean-Sébastian Rossbach
Ch. 3: Federico Dallocchino, Borkur Eiriksson
Ch. 4: Daniel Warren Johnson, David Palumbo

Comic Publisher: Dark Horse Comics
The game: EVE Online is a space-based, multiplayer online role-playing game released in 2003 and developed by CPP Games.
The Bloodbath of B-R5RB, set in the space game EVE Online in January 2014, lasted 21 hours with 200+ players and is possibly the player-versus-player largest battles in gaming history.

NOTES

1. https://www.darkhorse.com/Books/24-073/EVE-True-Stories-HC
2. https://www.goodreads.com/book/show/18853514-eve

CHAPTER 41

The new retail experience

Despite a recurring and consistent claim, the death of retail is largely exaggerated. At the time this book is being authored, the primary indicator for retail, sales, is in no way in decline.

The decline of retail should rather be phrased as the decline of sales in physical retail stores, their relevance to consumers decreasing to the point of retail brands closing stores or even going entirely out of business. Just a few years ago, many of the retail brands – some of the retail giants now gone or facing severe challenges – were seemingly everlasting. Some of them were considered too big to fail. However, even as we learned during the financial crisis that size does not ensure survival, many of these brands stayed on a course laid out many years ago without taking into serious consideration that their markets and customers were changing.

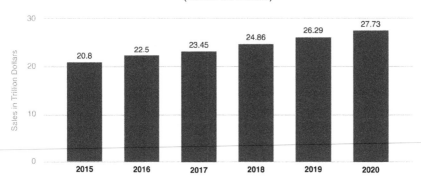

Global retail sales from 2015 to 2020 – 95% of all purchases are projected to be done via e-commerce.[1]

As businesses started realising that the post-financial crisis confronted them with adverse conditions that could be beyond resolution, the internet was singled out as the culprit and the reason why customers failed to show up in the physical stores.

However, if one takes a look at the evolution of retail and not at least how its role changes in the life story of their audiences, one can start identifying areas in which the detachment between retail and customers has been building since before the internet sales boom. Online shopping did, in many cases, widen the gap, but online services are a part of an evolution that has to be, if not anticipated, then at least used to rethink and reinvent any brand. Currently, the word used to describe technology-driven new business and as such, challenges to existing businesses, is Disruption. Not long after its popular adaption, the solution was named as Transformation of existing businesses and services.

Throughout the evolution of various industries and disciplines, disruptive shifts have happened that created a need for changing ways to stay relevant and avoid becoming outdated. This is nothing new, it has happened before, and it will happen again.

- Print technology disrupted the manufacturing of books.
- Photography disrupted art.
- Sound disrupted the silent-movie industry.
- Cars disrupted private transportation.
- Video recorders for home use disrupted the television and cinema industry.

The list goes on, with disruptions happening before print and after video recorders. With the computer, and consequently, the internet, a platform was created to disrupt all that came before and influence most that would follow. Adaption and transformation are imperative to become, and stay, successfully relevant. In transformative periods, while businesses and careers will be lost, new opportunities will arise as well.

We are in the midst of a fundamental evolution of retail, one where the very foundation and values – one might say DNA – of the modern-day retail has to change. As mentioned, customers are buying things, but retail can no longer be just about moving wares from one side of the counter to the other, whatever the transaction is virtual or physical. The focus for retail, at this point in time, has to be more about the retail experience. From the user experience of online shopping to the visitor experience of going to a store, shopping is more than the purchase of goods.

There are many approaches towards creating the new retail experience. They include leisure and entertainment in multiple ways to make visiting the retail space more alluring. However, unless the disciplines are genuinely integrated into a new experience, the outcome may be a fragmented, inconsistent customer experience, where the elements end up being superficial or even at odds with each other. Just because they are in the same place does not ensure that they are not out if place.

One of the critical elements in retail is the anchors, the stores and spaces that draw in customers. New anchors may be various experiences, but the different anchors need to be in balance as to support each other and avoid cannibalisation. In scenarios where the experience and the narratives as conveyed by the customers, not only the mall or the retailer, Integrated Storytelling can be applied as a valuable tool to ensure interdisciplinary integration along with a shared vision and understanding for an overall, complimentary retail experience.

INTEGRATED STORYTELLING FOR RETAIL

When using the principles of Integrated Storytelling for the new generation of retail, the Integrated Story Sphere can be applied to help define roles and characteristics for the retail customer encounter. One relevant scenario is that of the retail mall, as it holds many possibilities for multiple interactions. It should be noted that each mall should be considered unique and the elements and layers of the Integrated Story Experience have to be developed for each unique space.

At the core of it all, we have, of course, the audience, which in the case of retail should be considered as both customer and visitor, who obviously can interact with the environment. Interaction in the form of any kind of conversion or transaction is the intention, not just delivering a story combined with an experience. In the world of retail, measurements and accountabilities drive business. To meet that demand, we can add points of measurability throughout the audience journey. Points may include what Micro-Stories or Micro-Experiences are popular, even to the point of people wanting to pay for them, or how traffic is being motivated to move throughout the retail space.

When the Integrated Story Sphere is to be applied for retail, considerations regarding the audience and their experience include:

- Who is the audience, and why is this particular retail space relevant to them? Going beyond stating the usual target group thinking, but looking further with a more detailed look into the audience layers may unlock new possibilities.
- What is the core concept in terms of story and experience, and how does that relate to people? What makes – or can make – the story and the experience of the particular space unique, be it the stores, the locations, the community or something else.

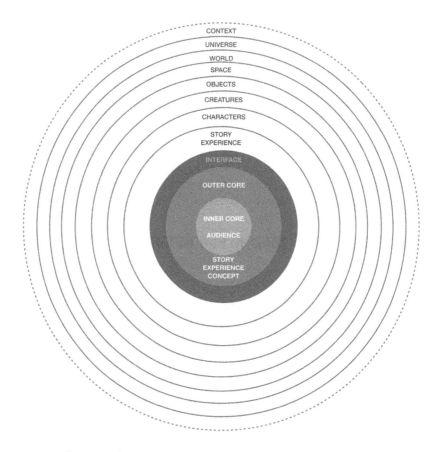

Integrated Story Sphere.

- How does the story come alive as an experience worth sharing with others? Developing the core concept further, how does it unfold as a story experience before, during and after the visit to the retail space?
- What kind of characters do people meet, and what roles do the characters have in support of the audience storyline? They may be hosts, store clerks, restaurant teams or something new completely. One may recognise that someone else is needed to complete the 'cast' of the retail experience.
- What kind of non-human creatures do they meet, and how does that relate to the overall story worth retelling? It could be a special place for animals, from domesticated pets to the animals in a store, mascots or virtual characters. Perhaps dinosaurs. Or, robots. There are many options, so it is imperative to remember that they should be relevant and interesting to well-defined groups of audiences.

- With which kinds of objects can they interact? Objects may obviously be wares, but once the design goes beyond the obvious objects, the space can become very intriguing.
- What are the different spaces that they move through throughout the story experience? Thinking in zones that accommodate various modalities may be vital to retaining them for more extended periods of time. Shopping and eating are just two; more can be added to create a nuanced experience space. Leaving room for people to just relax and chat without having to be activated or making a purchase, the so-called dwelling spaces, will also add to the length of how long people will stay in the retail space.
- What is the world that they are visiting? In this case, the world is the retail space, mall or individual store, and everything in it and around it that makes up the total experience from arrival to departure. Defining the retail world ensures consistency while still being able to present surprises.

Finally, there is the question of the overall audience context and relevance. For retail, the overall context goes beyond the space and creates a connection directly back to the audience layers to attract their attention and presence. In which context are they visiting the retail space? Is the reason a particular season or reason? Is it a social event? What effort does it take for them to get here? What is the balance between attraction and inconvenience? Understanding the context in which they experience the retail space can heavily influence how the Integrated Story Sphere should be constructed for this particular retail space.

NOTE

1. https://financesonline.com/retail-statistics/#global

CHAPTER 42

CASE: Søstrene Grene

The lifestyle retail franchise Søstrene Grene[1] stands out in many ways. The franchise has a storyline deeply rooted within the brand, and a store experience that goes beyond product and service has been at the heart of every Søstrene Grene store since the first one opened its doors in Aarhus, Denmark, in 1973. Since then, the brand has grown, since 1989 also as a franchise, and as of 2019, there were 245 stores in 16 countries. The brand is present online, at present with more than 1.5 million followers on Instagram,[2] which is dedicated to new collections, inspiration, Do-It-Yourself (DIY) tips, projects, etc. With a significant focus on the in-store experience, Søstrene Grene for a long time withheld the bold choice of not launching any e-commerce platform, which reportedly has not influenced overall sales. In 2020, though, Søstrene Grene has launched a web shop, countering the effect of continuous lockdowns due to the COVID-19 pandemic. This was planned well before the pandemic made its impact, though.

At the core of the Søstrene Grenes brand, we find two fictional characters, the elderly sisters Anna and Clara Grene, who have been with the brand since the first store was opened by Knud Cresten Vaupell Olsen and Inger Grene. The main characters in the story may be made up, but the family name is real, and to this day, the brand is owned and managed by the Grene family. The story premise about Anna & Clara is that they travel the world in their balloon – and in good spirit – to explore the world and bring back what they find, which is then sold in the stores. It is a kind-hearted story that no-one is expected to take too seriously; it embodies the spirit and the values of the brand which include joy, finds, creativity and the Danish concept of Hygge, which can be defined as a state of joy, satisfaction and cosiness.

The physical retail experience of Søstrene Grene makes the story, theme and values come alive with aesthetics and ever-changing presentations of the products. Visiting a store and walking its narrow aisles are immersive and sensory experiences, with the musical style carefully chosen

**VÆR MED TIL AT SKRIVE OG
TEGNE ÅRETS JULEKALENDER
OG VIND FLOTTE PRÆMIER!**

Se mere på www.grenes.dk.

**FINDER MANU, ANTON OG CARLA
DEN MYSTISKE PROFESSOR GRUHM?
OG KAN DE REDDE JULEN?**

Deltag i julekalenderen på www.grenes.dk

**SKRIV OG TEGN SLUTNINGEN
PÅ ÅRETS JULEKALENDER OG
VIND EN TUR TIL LALANDIA!**

Deltag på www.grenes.dk.

Throughout the years, Søstrene Grene has explored different formats of story-telling, including an online Christmas calendar co-created by Danish children.

and with the wares arranged uniquely in themes in the narrow aisles. It is a design that is carefully crafted for the primarily female audience.

Søstrene Grene has managed to merge story and experience, and proving it as a successful retail recipe well into the twenty-first century, growing as a retail brand in an otherwise challenged industry.

Søstrene Grene (English: The Grene Sisters) is a retail chain selling interior decor articles, gifts, stationery and furniture.
First store opened in 1973.
Location: The headquarters are situated in Aarhus. Since 1989, the company has been allowing the opining of franchises.
Founders: Knud Cresten Vaupell Olsen and Inger Grene. The chain is owned and operated by the second generation of the family, brothers Mikkel Grene (CEO) and Cresten Grene (Creative Director).

NOTES

1. https://sostrenegrene.com
2. https://www.instagram.com/sostrenegrene/

CHAPTER 43

Integrated Storytelling for Modern Marketing

Marketing and advertising are in a state of evolution, driven by technology advancement, customer empowerment, new consumer patterns and changes in the perception of the value of marketing efforts. As an example, broadcast television ads are one particular form of advertising that is increasingly perceived as less effective and costly compared to its impact. Consequently, advertising and marketing agencies are defining not only the positioning of their own businesses, but their industry in general. As a result, new disciplines and ways of creating attraction, action and sale are being explored as frantic solutions either to an industry crisis or as ways of innovating forward.

HOLISTIC APPROACHES TO MARKETING AND STORYTELLING

One of the coherent new concepts of marketing is that of Modern Marketing, a holistic approach spanning multiple disciplines. The definitions for it are as diverse as the agencies that present themselves as Modern Marketers. However, some points are consistent and can be used to define 10 points that define Modern Marketing as a general concept[1]:

EXPERIENCE: Modern Marketing elevates the brand experience at every touchpoint.
PERSONALISATION: Modern Marketing builds personalised connections with individuals.
TRANSMEDIA: Modern Marketing integrates omnichannel strategy and tactics.
DYNAMICS: Modern Marketing adapts to the evolution of the marketing landscape.

TECHNOLOGY: Modern Marketing maximises efficiency through technology.

MEASURABLES: Modern Marketing measures and analysis performance and data.

AGILITY: Modern Marketing leverages iterative execution and optimisation.

STRATEGY: Modern Marketing has a feedback-focused approach to strategy rather than a research-focused approach, making audience interaction and experimentation strategy-building activities.

AUDIENCE: Modern Marketing priorities audience brand perception and perspective over brand message and intention.

STORY: Modern Marketing applies customer journey-led narratives rather than brand-led narratives.

These ten points are easily relatable to the audience-centric story experiences designed with Integrated Storytelling principles:

EXPERIENCE: Integrated Storytelling is a design concept for creating story-based, themed and branded experiences.

PERSONALISATION: Integrated Storytelling can be used to find points of connection to adapt and customise the story experience to specific users or user groups.

TRANSMEDIA: Integrated Storytelling is a design method for creating narratives that span multiple platforms.

DYNAMICS: Integrated Storytelling principles are updatable and adaptable to new trends and achievements.

TECHNOLOGY: Integrated Storytelling can integrate and utilise both existing and upcoming technologies. Concepts created within the discipline are not defined by the limitations of a specific technology but are designed to be enhanced by both existing and upcoming technologies.

MEASURABLES: Integrated Storytelling can integrate points of measurability and data connection due to the modular structure containing points of audience interaction and influence.

AGILITY: Integrated Storytelling with its modular designs allow for various ways of updating objects and modules even while in operation. The complete structure does not have to be changed when making focused and isolated improvements or changes.

STRATEGY: Integrated Storytelling as a design method actively applies audience feedback from the early phases of creation in an audience-centric design structure that is integrated to be utilised at any later point, past launch and well into operations.

AUDIENCE: Integrated Storytelling is an audience-centric design method, with the perspective of design and development being that the audience.

STORY: Integrated Storytelling combines story and experience, with the audience perspective being the first perspective. Such is the case with the experiential narrative that is basically the intended story told by the audience.

CONTEMPORARY MARKETING DISCIPLINES

In extension to the Modern Marketing definitions above, different new marketing disciplines have emerged for new ways to utilise these key points to reach and engage a wider audience. Some of these are disciplines in their own right but should be recognised and considered by anyone working as or aspiring to work as a Modern Marketer.

Social media

The rise of social media has been explosive. It is by now widely adapted by billions around the world from different age groups, countries and cultures which in total numbers 3.5 billion daily users as of 2019,[2] even though the leading social media platforms have not been around that long in a media historical perspective – LinkedIn launched in May 2005, Facebook on 4 February 2004, YouTube in February 2005 and Twitter in March 2006. All of them initiated the worldwide adaption of social media, even though some of them are not globally accessible, e.g. LinkedIn is blocked in Russia, and YouTube is blocked in China.

Early social media strategies were often mass marketing strategies adopted to the new platforms, sometimes resulting in some unfortunate executions because of a lack of understanding of a particular platform's dynamics. One case being video ads delivered at unbearable lengths because YouTube provided a platform with less limitation in time and less need for media spending budgets than when advertising on television.

Some early successes, such as content going organically viral,[3] can be attributed to less content presented to a curious, new audience. This scenario is hard to replicate at this point, as along with the increased audience, an increased number of content providers and brands made the competition for audience interest and time considerably higher and more expensive.

Utilising social media draws upon several of the ten defining aspects of Modern Marketing. Even though it is easy to compare it to traditional televised advertising in terms of producing and uploading content, and if needed, spending a budget on promoting it for more views, one has to realise that social media is a vastly different context.

Here, everybody shares the same stage, and many are creators in their own right. That also means that original marketing content can end up as memes, video edits or get companionship by complementary, advocating videos as well as the opposite.

People can immediately comment and act to push their opinion about a new brand or product commercial, which can spread like wildfire, creating a groundswell effect[4] that will hardly let a brand know what hit it before the damage to public opinion is irreparable. More than anywhere else, online and on social media, the audience is in command, and just a single click or tap makes or breaks the chance for engaging them. In general, one has to remember that a social media platform is not a traditional media channel. It is a space for sharing and interacting that takes marketing past one-way communication and into a space where the interaction and discussion can become even very loud.

For the story creator and designer, beyond utilising technology and considering a strong audience perspective to the story told, designing for context and interaction is essential to fully utilise the potential of social media while proactively prepare for the discussion that may arise, as there may be polarised opinions and discussion in the wake of a post. Part of the creation of social media story experience is to create an anticipatory design that takes into account what should and what would not happen after the posting has been made. Was the purpose to begin a constructive discussion in line with a brand mission? Was it to inspire people to create something or share images or a hashtag that expands the brand recognition? Was it to make people reflect on and share their own stories? There are many more options than merely sharing a story and the balancing act is to find a way that will initiate a positive, constructive interaction and dialogue.

Storydoing

Storydoing is a relatively new practice in marketing and is an evolutionary step forward from creating content that is intended to go viral. When practising storydoing, the vital difference from storytelling is that compared to the latter, where a story creator tells a story on a chosen platform, storydoing inspires and enables people to tell the story in their own way on their chosen platform – or indeed, platforms. This approach speaks to the creative urge of many social media users, and the content created is authentic and honest, which can have a high impact on peers, as trust in family and friends and friends of friends is often stronger than that of brands. Even as people have learned that some peers are automated, robotic drivers or skewers of public opinion.

Working with storydoing is a highly innovative process, during which the designers need to create not a story, but a framework that will help drive the audience towards the role of story creation on their own. It may include sharing stories to inspire others to do, create and share their own stories, or provide them with all the elements they need to do so. Of course, some incentive has to exist to trigger the creation of an audience created story; why should they spend their time creating it?

Besides motivating the audience to do their own story, the framework also needs to provide them with a direction that supports the brand. This may be done through subtle nudging rather than direct instructions, to have the story created come through as personal, honest and authentic as possible. The story should not come through as a response to a briefing, or audiences will mentally label it as advertising. The story designer needs to consider what small elements such as stories and insights that need to be shared to create the direction, not dictating it.

Elements may include:

- Guidelines for creating an exciting story about topics that are relevant to the brand are shared to help in going from inspiration to action.
- Assets such as video, images and music that creates a connection to the brand are provided free of charge.
- Tools or platforms are offered for the creation and distribution of the story that the audience creates.
- Guidelines for uploading and distributing content on social media.

The point here is to make the creation and distribution as easy as possible while keeping the creative audience in control of their own story.

Experiential Marketing

The final example of a contemporary marketing discipline on this list is Experiential Marketing. It differs from the traditional mass-communication marketing, by not relying on the communicated, but the experienced message. Audiences can experience it first-hand or second-hand, with the latter also being capable in real-time through live streaming or similar.

The purpose of Experiential Marketing is to have the audiences experience the message through multiple senses, not just as an ad on television or in a magazine that at best combines sights and sounds. The unique experience becomes part of the personal narrative of each of the members of the audience. This ties into the social media and the storydoing disciplines above, as the memory of the experience becomes a shareable moment and a personal tale worth telling.

Experiential Marketing has a wider potential than being present with a booth at a sports game or doing a special after-hours sale for loyal customers, even as those kinds of events and have proven valuable many times. Experiential Marketing should be deeply rooted within the brand; it expands the brand narrative by making it come alive as an experience worth both living and sharing.

The Integrated Storytelling principles are relevant to Experiential Marketing because of the Story Sphere design with the combination of story and experience at the core, balancing the dynamics between the two. This balance ensures that an Experiential Marketing event does not become too much of a brand message without an experiential part, and that the event does not become an experience without no message or anchoring with the brand. Each of which does happen frequently. By maintaining and benefiting from the balance of story and experience, this can be avoided.

There are multiple similarities between creating story experience designs for Experiential Marketing and themed attractions. They both represent a storyline that is presented as an experience and they both let the audience walk through or live that experience in a physical space. Part of their spatial design is a strong theme or brand, which has the audience go through a version of a Hero's Journey-like structure. There is an entry, and adventure and an exit and the audience gets to bring something with them. That something may be intangible such as a memory, new knowledge or a story to share. It may also be very tangible such as merchandise or another object that shows brand advocacy. Working with Experiential Marketing places that are so heavily influenced by a brand will truly show if the story creators and designers can maintain a balance with the audience at the centre of the story experience. After all, the audience is the hero, and this experience is still their narrative, albeit in a brand theme and setting.

NOTES

1. https://www.oliveandcompany.com/blog/what-is-modern-marketing
   https://medium.com/part-and-sum/what-is-modern-marketing-what-must-marketers-prepare- for-3158db06ee5
2. https://www.oberlo.com/blog/social-media-marketing-statistics
3. Organically viral: when spreads fast online without being accelerated by any media spending
4. Josh Bernoff & Charlene Li: Groundswell (2011)

CHAPTER 44

CASE: Bleed for the throne

In April 2019, three strong brands came together to promote a cause that combined their position as entertainment phenomenon, well-established and well-respected NGO and as a stage for new innovations and technologies.

In partnership with the American Red Cross, HBO invited fans to prove their Game of Throne devotion and Bleed For The Throne. It was a gesture worthy of one of the biggest shows in television, and one designed to harness the cultural power of Westeros to help end blood shortages in the real world. Bleed For The Throne would become the most abundant blood donation promotional effort by an entertainment company in American Red Cross history, with six days of coordinated giving from fans across the entire country.

In addition to blood drives in 43 states and nine colleges and universities across the United States, the partnership included an immersive experience at SXSW (South by Southwest).[1] SXSW is an annual festival-like conference where people working in tech, film, music and more, all come together in Austin, Texas.

The audience at SXSW would cue up as donors or non-donors, and once entering the Game of Thrones house, would be able to immerse themselves in various storylines guided around using a set of headphone and an iPod touch with storylines based around Cersei, Arya, Jon and Tyrion.

Once people left this immersive experience, the audience could join the crowd in Great Hall to enjoy choir performances. During this time, red-clad women might come to the audience or call a batch by their names and ask them to queue in front of the iron throne. After kneeling in front of the red women, the audience could get the Hand of the King or Queen pin.

The Game of Thrones experience continued outside of the house. Dothraki, Wildlings, some fighters from Bear Island and more characters would interact with the audience and each other. Of course, the cast members were also available for photos with the audience.

Bleed For The Throne serves as not only an example of immersive Experiential Marketing, but also demonstrates how various existing brands, storylines and industries can be woven together by a shared story and purpose to create a new experience, rich on its own in multiple narrative designs and storylines.

Date: Immersive experience at SXSW from 7 to 9 March 2019 (Austin, Texas, U.S.)

American nationwide campaign in 43 states and nine colleges and universities across the United States from 7 to 12 March 2019.

The immersive experience was created in partnership with Giant Spoon.

According to HBO, on the first day of the nationwide campaign 15,000 pints of blood donations were collected.

More than 350,000 fans and blood donors in 43 out of 50 states answered the call for donations in February and March 2019.[2]

Fifteen other countries including Norway, Sweden, South Africa, Kenya, Ghana, Botswana, Hungary, Poland, Romania, Czech Republic, Bulgaria, Serbia, Greece and Croatia could participate in the events, organised by local blood donation organisations.

The collaboration between HBO and the American Red Cross continued in April 2019, giving the donors of that month the chance to win a full-size Iron Throne from HBO's Game of Thrones.

NOTES

1. SXSW (South by Southwest) https://www.sxsw.com
2. https://www.redcross.org/about-us/news-and-events/press-release/2019/american-red-cross-and-hbo-bleed-forthethrone-partnership.html

CHAPTER 45

Cases online

For an updated collection of cases, please visit:

IntegratedStorytellingByDesign.com

Futurecasting

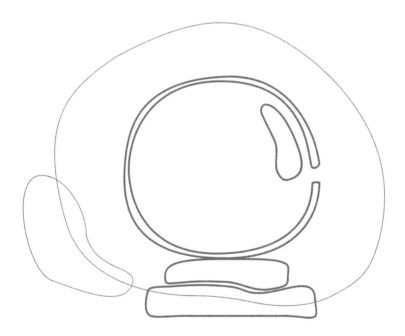

"The future influences the present just as much as the past."

Friedrich Nietzsche

CHAPTER 46

The future of the story experience

In some ways, storytelling is a time-travelling device. It allows us to leave our stories, fact or fiction, memory or legend to be explored and even relived by an audience for months, years, decades, centuries and even millennia in the future. It allows us to glance back to creators and authors who have left their stories and histories for later generations, letting us get closely connected with a girl named Anne hiding from the Nazi regime in an attic in Amsterdam,[1] or gaze across the thousands of years of the ancient Egyptian kingdoms. Storytelling allows us to dramatize and bend reality by sheer will, as what is perceived as history is presented by those who put it down in images and words.

> Storytelling allows us to dramatize and bend reality by sheer will.

A quarter of a century after Pine and Gilmore coined the Experience Economy,[2] bringing, among other things, principles that had been applied and somewhat confined to leisure and entertainment into other industries, and a quarter of a century after the average age of a Playstation user passed 21, the concepts of experience and gaming have come of age. They are no longer confined to a limited user group within a limited market, as the principles within are being applied widespread across industries including but not limited to learning, retail, marketing, healthcare, urban designs and, of course, the further evolution of entertainment and leisure both at home and out-of-home.

Storytelling and experience design are evolving. Their individual and collective future are, of course, still in a state of flux, but there are still some realistic future scenarios for the story creator and designer to take into consideration.

The following is not a definite list, and future predictions are, of course, always prone to individual opinions. As such, the list below exemplifies the trend initiators, which will most likely impact the evolution of the story experience.

THE NEXT BIG THING

In his book *The Next Big Thing*, William Higham[3] states that the vital trend initiators are:

Politics, e.g. policy, legislation and political events;
Economics, e.g. stability of needs, personal and national economy;
Society, e.g. health, schools and age; and
Technology, e.g. communications, transport and leisure.

For the story creator and designer, trends initiated by either of the above provide necessary considerations when defining the stories and the experiences that are in line with the meta trends that are shaping society and the regular lives of audiences. Sometimes, the initiators can influence one another, such as the impact that mobile devices (Technology) have had on our social behaviour (Society). To relate each of the four to storytelling, some recent impacts of the four trend initiators are:

Politics: The use of social media by the Barack Obama campaign arguably accelerated the global adaption of social media as a political and marketing discipline. Politics not only influences storylines and content presented, but also formats of the story experience. As is the case with Experiential Marketing, a political experience can also be a message to be experienced and not merely seen or heard.

Economics: Economic development, on a personal or national level, impacts the priorities of money spending; food and accommodation as a need outweigh the need for expensive pastime activities. However, in times of financial trouble on a larger scale, the need for escapism through leisure and entertainment also becomes evident, as is arguably presented through box office records still being made with a leniency towards the escapism genres: fantasy, science fiction and adventure in times of downturn economy.

Society: Successful storytelling creates a connection of relevance with current society, reflecting the issues within. For example, *An Inconvenient Truth* is a documentary from 2006 directed by Davis Guggenheim about former the United States Vice President Al Gore's campaign to educate people about global warming. While doing so, the documentary also made a societal impact and sparked a long-lasting debate about global warming.

Technology: Many of the new narrative possibilities in this book are driven by new technological achievements and their adaption by a widespread audience. The evolution of the story experience is not driven forward by one technology, but rather a convergence of technologies, how creators apply them and, most importantly, how the audience engages with them.

Mobile devices, in particular, the smartphone, have enabled the story experience to be presented anytime, anywhere without much preparation on the part of the audience. Mobile devices are currently being used for experiences beyond the podcast, the video and the audiobook such as location-based tours, missions, quests and marketing. We have still only seen the beginning of what the mobile story experience can be, even as they are explored in innovative ways by franchises like Harry Potter, Pokémon and Jurassic World.

The four trend initiators can be used to identify the different meta aspects influencing the future of the story experience. They can effectively be used to set the direction for how the wants and needs of the audience, and the needs and the purpose of the creator and the story can be combined to find the most successful overlap for future development of Integrated Storytelling.

THE FUTURE OF THE STORY EXPERIENCE IN A POLITICAL PERSPECTIVE

Political communication has changed monumentally with the widespread use of online and social media channels, often strongly opinionated and often automated, to the point of countries utilising bots and troll farms in overt cyber warfare to influence elections and public opinions. Even the highest-ranking politicians share their opinions unfiltered on platforms such as Twitter and Facebook, uprooting a system of controlled communication towards one of immediacy, emotion and opinion, often creating a causality chain in the process. The role of mainstream media is challenged and questioned, and media have become more polarised in some countries, reflecting the polarisation of the voters in said countries. The story of politicians and parties is very much created in the minds of the audiences as living examples of the multiple storylines that are part of an Integrated Storytelling design. However, the elements that make up the combined story are often an overly complicated, accidental series of endless Micro Stories with no coherent design; in laymen's terms, it is a noisy mess, leaving audiences to make sense of it all on their own. This opens up for polarised tales and the need for those who help make sense of it, which has redefined the role of the night-show host.

The critical elements of favourable storylines that create sympathy and goodwill towards a party, a cause or a candidate – or indeed the opposite – have consistently proven to be the power that storytelling can apply to politics. The future of communications, engagement and interaction in politics will require those professionals who are capable of crafting and presenting strong stories and use the right media in the process. In addition, it will, to a very high degree, require professionals who are capable of designing and operating a framework from which to maintaining control of the living story, as it is influenced and grown from various sources. The current social media tracking and response strategies are an early version of what will evolve in order to mass-customise the story. In some countries and regions of the world, that framework may very likely be one of responsive censorship based on pattern recognition from audience, voter and population observation.

THE FUTURE OF THE STORY EXPERIENCE IN AN ECONOMICAL PERSPECTIVE

In 2019, Disney had seven movies passing the $1 billion mark at the box office, with animated and live-action versions of previously animated features, *Marvel* and *Star Wars* movies making the list.[4] With Disney breaking its 2016 record significantly, the potential for vast profits from large-scale movies has pivoted larger studios towards big-budget productions. Many will argue that as far as cinematic releases are concerned, a considerable gap has appeared with small and indie productions on one end of the scale and multi-million budgets at the other, leaving little to no room for investment in the medium-sized movies in between the two.

However, there is a new platform available, albeit not for a full out-of-home cinematic experience. The subscription streaming services are in the early stages of a 'streaming war' and crave original content that drives subscriptions. For example, the traditional paid channel HBO has transformed into HBO Go and HBO Nordic. It was joined by Netflix, a DVD postal rental service that has transformed into a streaming platform and then into a content provider in its own right. Others include Amazon Prime, a range of app-based channels such as Curiosity Stream (Science) and The Design Network (Interior Design). Platforms such as YouTube, Facebook and Instagram are no longer solely focused on user-generated content and present original series. Recently, Disney has gone beyond their involvement in Hulu and entered the market with Disney +, a platform for original content and the comprehensive film and series archive of Disney productions, including acquisitions of *Marvel*, *Star Wars*, *Pixar* and FOX with an extended range of well-established and beloved franchises.

To the story creator and designer, the Streaming War opens up for opportunities in investments and innovation. Series like *Game of Thrones* (HBO), *Stranger Things* (Netflix) and *The Mandalorian* (Disney +) have proved the level of impact that can be made with streamed series. Furthermore, innovative approaches like Bandersnatch in the Dark Mirror series, an interactive branch-structured story, allows the audience to influence the direction of the story.

The story experience has to be developed further as an added value to the streaming service, which may move forward the evolution of the hybrid streaming service, positioned as being able to provide content situated somewhere in between games and movies.

As streaming services are already widely available across devices and platforms with content being watched on screens from smartphone sizes to large flat screens, and even with some Netflix movies now being presented in the platform's first cinema, the historic Paris cinema in New York, the streaming platforms are ready to move forward and become transmedia platforms. Productions would then have different formats, not just in terms of length and screen size, but also in terms of audience roles and influence, such as the possibility for interaction. This could move productions beyond the current 'produce one format to be applied anywhere' approach. Transmedia storytelling connected and tied to the streaming platform, could make it possible to enter, live and relive a favourite story in multiple ways without leaving out the option of simply watching it in a traditional, linear order as a passive audience.

THE FUTURE OF THE STORY EXPERIENCE IN A SOCIETAL PERSPECTIVE

This may be phrased as a social perspective, as the social experience is creating new possibilities across industries because of one simple and consistent truth: in general, people are social creatures, and experiences are richer when shared with someone; friends, family, acquaintances, even a group or a crowd of strangers at concerts and sports events.

People crave experiences and the need is met by an ever-expanding industry that includes theme parks, leisure, gaming, concerts, events, e-commerce, expanded realities, and new approaches towards retail and marketing evolving from being a message communicated to an experience orchestrated with an underlying message and/or incentive.

Other meta trends can be identified as tendencies towards catering to the social needs and further comfort to be in a space with both friends, family and strangers. Street food markets provide a different setting from the traditional restaurant, with tables being occupied by a mix of people, not a group of familiars secluded at one table or in a booth. New attractions and rides provide missions that are to be completed with groups made up of people that may be strangers. Such is the case of Smuggler's Run at Disney's Star Wars-themed Galaxy's Edge, where the visitors are given specific roles in order to make the Smuggler's Run with the Millennium Falcon successfully.

Obviously, how and to which extent we socialise and interact differs from person to person, culture to culture, country to country and region to region. Forcing a specific social aspect may backfire if not considering these differences. As a story designer and creator, keeping the audience layers and filters described in Part III well in mind may be what makes people engage with or avoid a particular story experience.

As presented with the meta trends above, which admittedly are based on North American, European and Russian observations, and as such should be given a fresh perspective when working in Asia, both business and leisure are pivoting towards more social experiences. It opens up possibilities for taking a fresh look at industries and experiences that have not fully defined the social aspects of their core experiences. This includes many retail brands, museums and learning institutions among others, which present designers and creators of Integrated Storytelling with opportunities for exploring and applying aspects such as social narrative designs and how they can be utilised to enhance or create shared social experiences. On a final, forward-looking note, coming out of the COVID-19 pandemic, work and workplaces may never be the same again with more work being done from home. In this setting, the need for establishing and maintaining a social connection between team members even when they are apart will become evident.

THE FUTURE OF THE STORY EXPERIENCE IN A TECHNICAL PERSPECTIVE

Technology, whether it is new production tools, programming capabilities, experience mechanics, digital media, quantum computing or something else, has a significant influence over the experience and evolution of storytelling. In a perfect – or even near-perfect balance between story, technology and experience, entirely new dimensions of a storyline can be unveiled, even creating new hybrid formats to explore storyworlds and storylines. When imbalanced, the technology may not be adequately applied in order to enhance the story. Reversely, infatuation with technology may leave the storyline and storyworld superficial and ultimately forgettable. The technical narrative design has to be in alignment with the story and the experience, while also taking the technical capabilities of the audience into consideration.

In the early–twenty-first century, technology has obtained a level of widespread adaption that makes it influence society. It can be argued that technology and society have not evolved at the same pace, with technology having accelerated beyond the societal evolution, not leaving enough time to adapt to appropriately and constructively assess the positive and negative impacts of technologies before they are deployed. Such a claim is frequently being made about social media in particular.

There is no doubt a long list of exciting and useful technologies coming up for the story creators and designers to be integrated into the production and audience experience of Integrated Storytelling in the immediate future. AI and XR are just two of the concepts worth mentioning as part of an array of rapidly expanding enhancement and possibilities that will be introduced.

The storyteller aspiring to be an Integrated Storytelling designer and creator, requires an understanding of emerging technologies and their potential to be widely adopted by the audience who is capable of making an impact on storylines in particular and on storytelling in general.

The future of The Story Experience in a Technical Perspective is not just about new technology features; it is about ensuring their relevance and adoption to implement them to enhance storytelling successfully. With that sentiment setting the direction, not only will the story experience evolve, but also its underlying mechanics and development. This may pave the way for more visionary ways of letting people experience a story, such as personal adaption and customisation.

On this next stage of the evolution of storytelling, new advancements in strategy, design and creation will emerge and come together to provide the inner and outer workings of the convergence of story and experience.

NOTES

1. Anne Frank: The Diary of a Young Girl (1995)
2. B. Joseph Pine II and James H. Gilmore: The Experience Economy (2011)
3. William Higham: The Next Big Thing, Kogan Page (2009)
4. https://www.businessinsider.com/disney-movies-with-1-billion-at-box-office-2019-8

Afterword

"Life can only be understood backwards, but it must be lived forwards."

Søren Kierkegaard

CHAPTER 47

Storytelling is not what storytelling was

Storytelling is not what storytelling was, and the role of the story creator is in a state of constant evolution; it will branch out into various roles and gain different focuses, merging even more disciplines. New ways of thinking and working will be developed, and with them, strategic and creative tools and principles that help bring the evolution of storytelling forward through invention and implementation. We are all at the campfire, discussing and exploring what our craft can become.

INTEGRATED STORYTELLING IS A CONCEPT WITH MANY FINGERPRINTS

The principles and methods in this book were not developed in the vacuum of the study of the secluded thinker. They were developed, introduced, reviewed, revisited and redesigned in a continuous cycle of discussion and

deployment around the world. Development and discussion in collaborative teams helped make them what they are today.

Everyone who joined the discussion, whether they were students and professionals from Denmark. Moldova, Canada, the United States, the United Kingdom, Russia, Estonia, Australia, Hong Kong – or somewhere else, the list goes on – has somehow left their fingermark through questions and comments, and by adding just a little more cultural perspective.

Furthermore, as this book came about, interaction with editors and reviewers has also influenced and impacted the evolution of the Integrated Storytelling discipline as presented on these pages. The story about Integrated Storytelling is, in itself, an example of a living story, where audiences have left their mark.

STEPPING FORWARD INTO THE FUTURE OF STORY DESIGN

At this point, what the future of storytelling is lies obscured. However, production and distribution accessibility, new technologies and innovative ways of designing and creating story experiences do point to a vision of what is to come; one where the creator and audience are in interchangeable roles, and where being a creator is not an exclusive role, but where the individualised story experience may feel exclusive.

Those who venture beyond traditional storytelling are about to embark on a journey that sometimes may be reserved for the bold and the brave. Pioneers at the frontline will face challenges. However, they will also continue to evolve themselves as well as their discipline of story experience design and creation. The level of interdisciplinary skillsets and insights it will take to do this successfully will almost certainly have a new group of innovative groups of story professionals and artist take the stage. To thrive, evolve and expand as a group, they will need training and possibilities to carry out their visions as real-life productions. Their progress will depend on how well decision-makers across industries and academic institutions understand the new possibilities that are emerging.

BENDING THE RULES

Initiatives like this book are created to support the evolution of storytelling towards that of new ways of designing, create and experiencing stories through suggestion rather than dictation. The design strategies, disciplines and models presented here are not a formula or definite descriptions of how to work with Integrated Storytelling. Of course, they can be immediately applied wherever the story and the experience in convergence can fulfil a purpose and make a significant difference to both creators and audiences, and whomever else may benefit. However, anything found on these pages can also be further developed and customised for specific projects and purposes, as new scenarios may present new challenges and opportunities. Doing so is not breaking the rules that will continue to evolve anyway. Those who take these steps forward will be doing so according to the nature of innovation and design, to meet any challenge and opportunity by developing, testing and implementing solutions that may unlock doors to hidden treasures.

Your journey has just begun.

Literature and media list

LITERATURE AND MEDIA LIST

Books

Anderson, C. (2017). *TED Talks: The Official TED Guide to Public Speaking.* Boston: Houghton Mifflin Harcourt.

Atwood, M. (2017). *The Handmaid's Tale.* London: Vintage.

Berger, A. M. (2013). *Every Guest Is a Hero – Disney's Theme Parks and the Magic of Mythic Storytelling.* Orlando: BCA Press.

Bernoff, J., Li, C. (2011). *Groundswell, Expanded and Revised Edition: Winning in a World Transformed by Social Technologies.* Boston, MA: Harvard Business Review Press.

Brown, T. (2019). *Change by Design: How Design Thinking Transforms Organizations and Inspires Innovation (Revised, Updated).* New York: Harper Business.

Campbell, J. (1949). *The Hero with a Thousand Faces.* New York: Pantheon Books.

Carroll, L. (1865). *Alice's Adventures in Wonderland.* London: Macmillan.

Christopher, J. (1988). *The Tripods Trilogy.* USA: Simon & Schuster.

Cockerell, L. (2008). *Creating Magic: 10 Common Sense Leadership Strategies from a Life at Disney.* USA: Doubleday.

Edginton, I., D'Israeli. (2006). *H.G. Well's War of the Worlds.* USA: Dark Horse Comics.

Frank, A., Frank, O., Pressler, M., Massotty, S. (1995). *The Diary of a Young Girl: the definitive edition.* New York: Doubleday.

Gadney, G. (2019) *Stepping Through The Screen.* In: K. S. Paulsen, ed. *Storytelling Beyond The Screen.* Aarhus: Filmby Aarhus/VIA Film & Transmedia/Create Converge – European Union North Sea Region VB programme, pp. 84–91.

Heath, D., Heath, C. (2017). *The Power of Moments: Why Certain Experiences Have Extraordinary Impact.* New York: Simon & Schuster.

Higham, W. (2009). *The Next Big Thing: Spotting and Forecasting Consumer Trends for Profit.* London: Kogan Page Limited.

Kim, A. J. (2018). *Game Thinking: Innovate Smarter & Drive Deep Engagement with Design Techniques from Hit Games.* Burlingame: Gamethinking, IO.

Lenderman, M. (2007). *Experience the Message: How Experiential Marketing Is Changing the Brand World*. New York: Basic Books.

Lukas, S. (2012). *The Immersive Worlds Handbook: Designing Theme Parks and Consumer Spaces*. Abingdon: Routledge.

McMakin, T., Fletcher, D. (2018) *How Clients Buy: A Practical Guide to Business Development for Consulting and Professional Services*. Wiley.

Miller, D. (2017). *Building a Storybrand: Clarify Your Message So Customers Will Listen*. Nashville: HarperCollins Leadership.

Newport, C. (2016). *Deep Work: Rules for Focused Success in a Distracted World*. New York: Grand Central Publishing.

Pine, B. J., Gilmore, J. H. (2011). *The Experience Economy, Updated Edition*. Boston, MA: Harvard Business Review Press.

Porter, N., ed. (1913). *Webster's Revised Unabridged Dictionary*. Springfield, MA: C. & G. Merriam Co.

Ritskes, R., Ritskes-Hoitinga, M. (2006). *Endorfiner*. Gjern: Bogan.

Smith, J. H., Tosca, S. P., Egenfeldt-Nielsen, S. (2008). *Understanding Video Games: The Essential Introduction*. London: Routledge.

Storr, W. (2020). *The Science of Storytelling: Why Stories Make Us Human and How to Tell Them Better*. New York: Abrams Press.

Verne, J. (1864). *Voyage au centre de la Terre (Journey to the Center of the Earth)*. France: Pierre-Jules Hetzel.

Verne, J. (1870). *Vingt mille lieues sous les mers: Tour du monde sous-marin (Twenty Thousand Leagues Under the Sea: A World Tour Underwater)*. France: Pierre-Jules Hetzel.

Verne, J. (1873). *Le Tour du monde en quatre-vingts jours (Around the World in Eighty Days)*. France: Pierre-Jules Hetzel.

Way, D. (2014) *EVE: True Stories*. Dark Horse Books.

Wells, H. G. (1895). *The Time Machine*. UK: Heinemann.

Wells, H. G. (1896). *The Island of Doctor Moreau*. UK: Heinemann.

Wells, H. G. (1897). *The Invisible Man*. UK: C. Arthur Pearson.

Wells, H. G. (1898). *The War of the Worlds*. UK: William Heinemann.

Blog post

Kaire, S. Writers Store *5 High Concept Requirements Defined Once and For All* [blog] Available at https://www.writersstore.com/high-concept-defined-once-and-for-all/ [Accessed December 21 2020]

Games

Cyan Worlds (1993) Myst. 1993. [Video game, MAC OS] Broderbund, USA.

id Software. (1993, 1994, 2004, 2005, 2012, 2016, 2020) Doom (series) [Video game franchise] id Software, USA.

Insomniac Games (2002-present), High Impact Games (2007-2008), Sanzaru Games (2009), Nihilistic Software (2012-2013), Tin Giant (2012), Mass Media (2014) Ratchet & Clank (series) [Video Game, PlayStation 2-5, Android, iOS] Sony Interactive Entertainment.

Maxis (1989) SimCity. [Video game, AMI, MAC, PC, C64, FMT, X68, PC98, CPC, ST, ARCH, BBC] Maxis, USA.
Maxis (2000) The Sims. [Video game, Microsoft Windows] Electronic Arts, North America.
Mojang (2011) Minecraft. [Video game, Windows, OS X, Linux] Mojang, Sweden.
Namco (1980) Pac-Man. [Game, Arcade] Namco, Japan.
Other Ocean Interactive. (2011) The War of the Worlds. [Video game, Xbox 360, PlayStation 3] Paramount Digital Entertainment, Other Ocean Interactive, USA.
Rage Software. (1998) Jeff Wayne's The War of the Worlds [Video game, Microsoft Windows] GT Interactive, USA.
Rockstar Games (2018) Red Dead Redemption 2. [Video game, PlayStation 4, Xbox One, Microsoft Windows, Stadia] Rockstar Games, USA
Taito (1978) Space Invaders. [Game, Arcade] Taito, Japan.

Movies and TV series

An Inconvenient Truth. [Film] Directed by Davis Guggenheim. Participant Productions, USA, 2006.
Behind the Curve. [Documentary film] Directed by Daniel J. Clark. Delta-v Productions, USA, 2018.
Black Mirror: Bandersnatch. [Film] Directed by David Slade. House Of Tomorrow, Netflix, UK, 2018.
Close Encounters of the Third Kind [Film] Directed by Steven Spielberg. EMI Films, UK, 1977.
E.T. the Extra-Terrestrial. [Film] Directed by Steven Spielberg. Universal Pictures, USA, 1982.
From Dusk till Dawn. [Film] Directed by Robert Rodriguez. Miramax, USA, 1996.
Kingdom [TV series] Directed by Kim Seong-hun (season 1). AStory, South Korea, 2019-.
Once Upon a Time in America. [Film] Directed by Sergio Leone. The Ladd Company, Warner Bros., USA, 1984.
Our Planet. [Documentary series] Silverback Films, USA, UK, 2019.
Psycho. [Film] Directed by Alfred Hitchcock. Shamley Productions, USA, 1960.
Star Wars: Episode IV – A New Hope. [Film] Directed by George Lucas. Lucasfilm Ltd., USA, 1977.
Star Wars: Episode V – The Empire Strikes Back. [Film] Directed by Irvin Kershner. Lucasfilm Ltd., USA, 1980.
The Birth Of A Nation. [Film] Directed by David Wark Griffith. David W. Griffith Corp., USA, 1915.
The Matrix 4. [Film] Directed by Lana Wachowski. NPV Entertainment, USA, 2021.
The Matrix Reloaded. [Film] Directed by Lana Wachowski , Lilly Wachowski. Warner Bros, USA, 2003.
The Matrix Revolutions. [Film] Directed by Lana Wachowski, Lilly Wachowski. Warner Bros, USA, 2003.

The Matrix. [Film] Directed by Lana Wachowski (as The Wachowski Brothers), Lilly Wachowski (as The Wachowski Brothers). Warner Bros, USA, 1999.

The Triumph of the Will. [Film] Directed by Leni Riefenstahl. Leni Riefenstahl-Produktion, Reichspropagandaleitung der NSDAP, Germany, 1935.

The Usual Suspects. [Film] Directed by Bryan Singer. PolyGram Filmed Entertainment, Bad Hat Harry Productions, Blue Parrot, Spelling Films International. USA 1995.

The War of the Worlds. [Film] Directed by Byron Haskin. Paramount Pictures, USA, 1953.

The War of the Worlds. [TV series] Mammoth Screen, British Broadcasting Corporation (BBC), Creasun Media American, UK, 2019.

Titanic. [Film] Directed by James Cameron. Twentieth Century Fox, Paramount Pictures. USA, 1998.

War of the Worlds 2: The Next Wave. [Film] Directed by C. Thomas Howell. Anthill Productions, USA, 2008.

War of the Worlds: Goliath. [Film] Directed by Joe Pearson. Tripod Entertainment, Malaysia, 2012.

War of the Worlds. [Film] Directed by David Michael Latt. The Asylum, USA, 2005.

War of the Worlds. [Film] Directed by Steven Spielberg. Paramount Pictures, Dreamworks Pictures, USA, 2005.

War of the Worlds. [TV series] Created by Greg Strangis. Hometown Films, Paramount Television, Ten Four, Triumph, USA, Canada, 1988–1990.

Music

Wayne, J. (1978) Jeff Wayne's Musical Version of The War of the Worlds [Vinyl] UK: Columbia/CBS Records.

Papers

Boje, D. M. (2012) What is Living Story Web?. Available at: https://davidboje.com/Boje/What%20is%20Living%20Story.htm [Accessed December 21 2020]

Rauscher, A. (2012) Video Game Genres - Typology [pdf] Available at: https://www.academia.edu/10376283/Video_Game_Genres_Typology   [Accessed December 21 2020]

Think with Google (2012) The New Multi-screen World: Understanding Cross-platform Consumer Behaviour. [pdf] Available at https://www.thinkwithgoogle.com/marketing-strategies/app-and-mobile/the-new-multi-screen-world-study/ [Accessed December 21 2020]

Radio shows

'The War of the Worlds' The Mercury Theatre on the Air [Radio programme] Directed by Orson Welles. USA, 19:00, 31 October 1938, CBS Radio, 60 mins.

INTEGRATED STORYTELLING BY DESIGN

Online literature and media

For an updated collection of literature and media, please visit

IntegratedStorytellingByDesign.com

Index

Lightning Source UK Ltd.
Milton Keynes UK
UKHW022346130722
405829UK00007B/33

9 780367 856977